Confluence

NOT

Coincidence

Confluence
NOT
Coincidence

USING THE POWER OF TECHNOLOGY TO HELP IDENTIFY MARKET DRIVERS IN TRADING AND INVESTING

PAUL BRATBY

Niche Pressworks
Indianapolis, IN

Confluence Not Coincidence

Copyright © 2023 by Paul Bratby

Published by Niche Pressworks; NichePressworks.com
Indianapolis, IN

ISBN
Paperback: 978-1-952654-97-8
eBook: 978-1-962956-03-1

To my dear grandson Logan, you have been more than just a "big help" during the summer of 2023. Your presence and enthusiasm for having fun in Spain with your grandma and me was truly a highlight of my year. I will be forever grateful for the memories we created together. Moreover, your unique perspective as an 11-year-old was invaluable to me as a writer, helping me to break through barriers and approach my book with renewed clarity. Through your eyes, I saw the world in a different way, and it inspired me to concentrate on keeping explanations simple.

And, of course, my darling wife Dee, who has been a constant support during my trading career and beyond. It's not easy being a trader's wife, and I thank you for your patience and emotional support to follow my dreams.

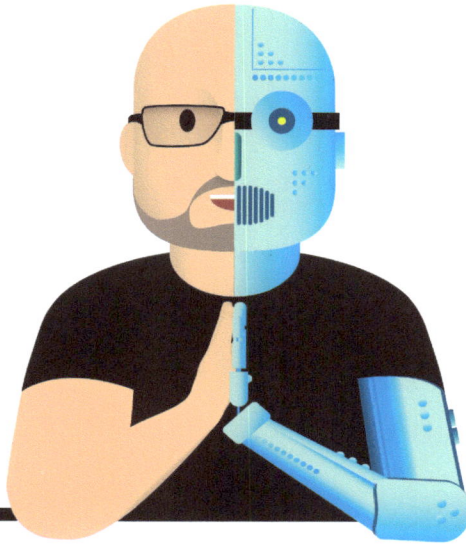

As gratitude for purchasing my book, I would like to give you
2 of my trading software titles that I mention in this book.

Simply Scan the QR code below for more information.

Scan me!

Table of Contents

Preface

THERE'S ONLY ONE thing better than trading — Formula One. Many people think it's just a bunch of expensive, loud cars ripping around a track, but that's only partially true. I love that F1 is an incredibly strategic sport driven by statistical data. Every team, from Ferrari to McLaren, relies on team strategists who use mathematical models and probability matrices to determine the route that will get them the best possible finish for their cars.

By the time the driver hits the track, these behind-the-scenes strategists have done the math and created multiple plans that take into consideration everything from weather, fuel, and tyre degradation to the deployment of safety cars and historical data. This statistically based race strategy informs every choice on the track. What seems like a big decision during a race is usually based on multiple decisions that have already been made.

For me, F1 is actually a lot like trading. But I didn't always approach trading in such a methodical way. It took time for me to work out my strategy. It all started in the late 1990s while I was attending a very technical engineering course on hydraulic and electronic systems whilst in the British Army.

Throughout the class, I was transfixed by the patterns of flow when certain demands were put on systems.

At the same time, I was trading at night to make some extra money and to set myself up for what I would do when I eventually left the army. I started by trading currencies on the foreign exchange (forex) market. This was a great way to start because it was pretty straightforward and easily accessible, and I could trade after hours.

I spent countless hours trying to figure out forex trading charts when, suddenly, something just clicked. I zoomed out and started to see patterns of flow on the trading charts that looked a lot like the systems and patterns of flow I was studying in my training course. But I didn't yet know what these patterns meant. Back then, I didn't even know the correct terminology used in the trading world.

For example, I could tell there was up movement in the charts followed by down movements, and this pattern seemed to repeat, following a similar pattern. Until it didn't. The pattern broke, and at that time, I didn't know why. I was frustrated. My next mission targeted understanding this movement and why the pattern deviated. Zooming out further, I kept seeing the pattern repeated regularly and figured there must be a reason. I became laser-focused on finding that reason and determining what was causing the changes.

I realized that many of the spikes occurred right after Europe and the US sent out their economic data releases. This really caught my attention. Things were making some sense — but not complete sense. Not all economic data points caused the same reaction, which was perplexing because there didn't seem to be a constant reason or pattern.

It was then that I started focusing on all the factors that impact the market. This was a big breakthrough because I started to understand confluence as it relates to trading. I was already familiar with the concept of confluence as it was used a lot in my engineering course. In that context, I was taught that confluences were "hydraulically complex fluvial systems of two or more confluent channels amalgamating into one downstream channel, resulting in rapid changes in flow." I know those are a lot of words. To make it a little less engineering techy, an example from nature may help. Think of small rivers and countless tributaries converging at various points and eventually merging into a main river. As this merging process progresses, the river grows in size and gains momentum. Each smaller element impacts the others and results in something different and new.

In trading, those small rivers and tributaries are the multiple data points that influence the market. That stuck with me. It made sense. Multiple factors (or confluences) combine to create patterns. I realized I had the ability to see and identify patterns that could help me make smart trading decisions.

This understanding sparked my passion. It's the beginning of my story and how I got hooked on trading and developing tools to help other traders.

Introduction

LET'S START BY talking about the title — *Confluence Not Coincidence*. Confluence is not about chance, and it goes beyond mere coincidence. A confluence occurs when two or more factors align to confirm a trend or reversal, and it is a powerful tool that can help traders and investors navigate the complex and dynamic world of financial markets.

I learned to trade the hard way, and I wrote this book so you don't have to learn like I did. The book provides readers with a resource of the best parts of what I've learned in my 20+ years of experience.

In the following chapters, we will discuss the principles surrounding trading and investing. We'll delve into two types of trading and strategies — day trading futures and swing trading or investing in stocks. With day trading, you buy and sell in the same day in hopes of capitalizing on small price movements. Swing trading involves holding positions for a longer time, days or even weeks, to try to profit from larger price movements.

Throughout the book, I will focus on the impact of patterns as well as tools and strategies that can help you identify these patterns and confluences in the market — and also help you make informed investment decisions.

XBRAT TECHNOLOGY

A lot has changed since I started trading. Early on, I had to scour charts and financials to look for patterns I knew were there. Technology and the development of high-speed computing systems have revolutionized how financial markets operate. Algorithms are now a fundamental part of trading and investing. They consolidate massive amounts of information, which can then be used to analyse data, monitor market trends, and execute trades. Those things together allow for quicker decisions and improve profits.

Despite all these advances, it wasn't until 2013 that technology was finally advanced enough for me to start the next journey in my life — developing software solutions that made it possible for me (and now all traders) to become consistently profitable in the markets without spending a decade learning (and losing money in the process).

Throughout the book, you'll notice I talk a lot about my xBrat software. I focused on building products designed around trading strategies that I developed after years of profitable trading. There are other products out there, but I believe the xBrat technology will transform your trading forever. I use the software myself every day, and it consistently delivers results for me, so that's why I've used it in examples to illustrate different trading strategies.

I've organized the book into four sections and included a Trading Terms glossary at the end of the book. In brief, the sections are organized as follows:

SECTION 1 –
UNDERSTANDING CONFLUENCES

Discover the art of comprehending and identifying confluences that arise from the convergence of multiple technical indicators, fundamental factors, or external events. Confluences hold the power to potentially indicate a shift in market direction, making them crucial for astute interpretation.

SECTION 2 –
CATALYSTS AND CONFLUENCE

Gain valuable knowledge on how to proficiently identify which catalysts have the potential to enhance the confluence or lead to its breakdown in the dynamic and ever-changing financial markets. By understanding these key factors, you can navigate through the complexities of the market with confidence and make informed decisions.

SECTION 3 –
CONFLUENCE AND TRADING STRATEGIES

Learn powerful and effective day trading, swing trading, and investing strategies that incorporate the concept of confluence. These strategies encompass a range of techniques to help you navigate the financial markets with confidence and make informed decisions. Whether you are a beginner or an experienced trader, mastering these strategies will equip you with the knowledge and skills to achieve your financial goals.

4

SECTION 4 –
CONCLUSION AND NEXT STEPS

Reflect on what we've covered and prepare to take the next steps. This section includes some handy confluence checklists for day trading, swing trading, and investing. These lists will equip you with essential tools to identify and evaluate opportunities effectively, allowing you to make informed decisions and optimize your trading and investment activities.

By focusing on confluence, readers will gain a deeper understanding of market trends, identify profitable opportunities, and make more informed trading decisions. The book is an invaluable resource for anyone seeking to improve their trading knowledge and unlock the full potential of their trading and investing.

Today, I trade with confidence using a simple and repeatable trading strategy while teaching thousands of traders how to trade with consistent profits for themselves. I can teach you to identify confluences and use technology to enhance your trading and investing.

A WORD ABOUT SPELLING ...

Whilst reading this book, you'll likely notice some words with different behaviours. Don't look on them unfavourably or overanalyse. It's simply that I've used British English throughout the book because I grew up in the United Kingdom, and that's the way it's done there.

SECTION 1

UNDERSTANDING CONFLUENCES

CHAPTER 1

Confluences and Financial Markets

FINANCIAL MARKETS ARE, by definition, highly unpredictable and subject to a variety of influences — both internal and external. However, confluences can help traders see connections in this seemingly chaotic environment. A confluence occurs when two or more factors come together, which can signal a potential change in market direction. When these factors align, the impact of each individual factor is amplified, and this synergy signals something to watch.

It is often said that there are no coincidences in the financial markets. Every outcome comes from the complex confluence of historical data and various external factors (like political and environmental events, stock sectors, etc.) that interplay and influence market behaviour.

To help navigate these factors, traders and investors utilize a range of trading indicators and associated strategies designed to work in different market conditions. By using various indicators and strategies together, traders can gain a more comprehensive understanding of the market and build confidence in their trading decisions.

It is essential to highlight that decision-making in the financial markets is primarily based on analysis, research, and experience. To become successful in this complex system, it is crucial that traders carefully evaluate their trading strategies, constantly refine their skills, and stay up to date with market conditions.

IDENTIFYING CONFLUENCE

In financial markets, confluence refers to the convergence of multiple technical indicators, fundamental factors, or a myriad of external events. The combination of these factors can signal a potential change in market direction or confirm a market trend or reversal. Essentially, confluence combines multiple strategies and ideas into one complete strategy.

I like to think of confluence as my "perfect storm" locator — a combination of factors that come together to create a confluence, indicating that a market is either extremely favourable or extremely unfavourable. In the case of a favourable market, it would indicate that everything is aligned in a positive way, signalling that it might be a good time to act. In an unfavourable market, it's time to proceed with extreme caution or stay out of the market completely.

Traders and investors rely on confluences to provide strong signals on market direction, which can help increase the probability of successful trades. However, it is important to understand that confluences can occur at any time within a market, and it is up to the individual trader to identify and act on them.

TECHNICAL ANALYSES

In technical analyses, a confluence can be identified through the analysis of multiple indicators, such as moving averages, trend lines, support and resistance levels, and various chart patterns. When these indicators align, indicating the same trend, it can strengthen the validity of the trend and help traders make more informed trading decisions.

FUNDAMENTAL FACTORS

Fundamental factors, on the other hand, are based on elements such as economic releases, central bank statements, political events, and other market-moving news. When multiple fundamental factors align, it can provide a strong signal for market direction and help traders anticipate potential market moves.

Identifying confluences can often be a complex process, requiring a thorough understanding of market dynamics as well as technical and fundamental analyses. However, by keeping a close eye on market trends and utilizing the right tools and indicators, traders and investors can increase their chances of making successful trades.

EXTERNAL FACTORS

In addition to technical analysis and fundamental factors, any number of external factors can also play an important role in identifying confluences. Among the most crucial external factors that shape financial market behaviour are world events and environmental occurrences.

Political events, war, natural disasters, and global pandemics can have a significant impact on financial markets. For example, the recent COVID-19 pandemic had an adverse impact on the stock markets across the world, leading to significant declines in major indexes worldwide.

Economic data and political structures are crucial external factors that influence financial market behaviour. Economic data, such as gross domestic product (GDP), inflation, and interest rates, can have a significant impact on the financial markets. Political structures, such as government policies and regulations, trade agreements, and geopolitical tensions, also play a critical role in shaping market behaviour.

The 2020 US presidential election is a good example of how political events can affect market behaviour. The contested election and its aftermath led to a significant level of uncertainty among investors, causing volatility and fluctuations in the markets. As the election results became clear, the market rallied based on expected shifts in the country's economic and political policies.

Another critical factor that affects market behaviour is the **demand and supply of commodities**, including oil, gold, and silver, which have a direct impact on economies across the world. For instance, the price of oil can have a direct and significant impact on the value of the currencies associated with oil-producing countries.

Stock sectors also play a crucial role in shaping financial market behaviour. Different sectors, such as energy, healthcare, technology, and financials, have unique characteristics, and they respond differently to external factors. A change in regulations in any one sector can have a ripple effect on other related sectors.

EXTERNAL FACTOR: WEATHER

Financial markets and nature are intertwined and generally exist in a state of balance. However, unexpected events and natural disasters can occur and upend this equilibrium. In the financial markets, unexpected events result in volatility that can impact markets.

Hurricanes in Florida are a good example of how natural events can impact the financial markets. During hurricane season, the stock prices for home improvement companies like Home Depot and Lowes perform exceptionally well. This is especially true right after a hurricane when extensive rebuilding occurs. Caterpillar, a construction equipment company, has also had its stock prices increase after hurricanes. When I identify these events occurring, I always try to swing trade and look for confluences in $HD, $LOW, or $CAT.

An inverse confluence that occurs in this equation is an immediate decline in insurance companies' stock prices. Insurance companies are paying out claims to fund repairs, so an initial decline is inevitable. But it's important to note that insurance company stocks are generally great buys, which makes this price dip a buying opportunity for investors. Once the disaster is over and claim payouts are more measurable, premiums begin to rise again, and these companies' revenue streams improve. Ultimately, their stock prices rebound. When I see this inverse confluence, I personally look to buy $AIG and $CB.

DECISION-MAKING AND CREATING RULES

A confluence strategy can help traders improve their decision-making skills and trading outcomes. Rather than getting overwhelmed with information and details, a confluence approach helps them look for synergies that signal something relevant —favourable or unfavourable.

When unfavourable confluences occur, traders can safeguard themselves by creating "safety net" rules within their trading strategies and sticking to them. This might include things like setting stop loss orders, limiting the amount of money that can be invested in any one trade, or avoiding trades that don't meet certain criteria. By adhering to these rules, traders can maintain discipline and avoid making impulsive decisions that could lead to losses.

The presence of unfavourable confluences is also important to note when considering a trade because it represents multiple factors that have combined to create a high-risk environment. For example, a major economic event like a recession or a political crisis could cause multiple markets to crash at the same time, which would be an unfavourable confluence for traders.

In such situations, it may be tempting to try to take advantage of the volatility by making risky trades. However, this is precisely the kind of behaviour that should be avoided. Rather than trying to profit from the chaos, traders should instead look for indicators that provide reasons "not to trade." Instead of jumping into the chaos, the best course of action is to identify and avoid trades that could be too risky in the current environment or, better yet, wait until the markets stabilise.

It's worth noting that unfavourable confluences are not always easy to predict, and there will be times when even the most disciplined traders will take losses. However, by focusing on risk management and avoiding unnecessary risks (by sticking to the rules), traders can minimise their losses and maximise their chances of success over the long term.

SIMILARITIES TO OTHER SECTORS

The success of any investor or trader depends on their ability to analyse and understand the dynamics of the financial markets. To explain the elements of financial markets in a different way, I thought it might be helpful to point out similarities to other sectors you may be familiar with. To this end, we'll briefly discuss similarities between the financial markets and specific sectors — nature, society, engineering, and computing. It's interesting to see how they have similar behaviours, structures, and rules.

NATURE

Both financial markets and nature embody the concept of evolution. In the natural world, evolution refers to the gradual development and adaptation of species over time. Similarly, the financial markets are never static, and they evolve constantly in response to various factors or influences, such as the advancement of technology that facilitates trading and investing, changing regulatory frameworks, and shifts in consumer preferences.

SOCIETY

Financial markets and social institutions both rely on order and frameworks to function. Society has laws and regulations, and financial markets have strict regulatory frameworks. These frameworks are often put in place to protect investors from fraud, market manipulation, and illegal activities that could compromise the stability of the markets.

ENGINEERING

Financial markets are engineered systems meant to facilitate trading and investing. Similarly, engineering is the application of scientific knowledge to design and develop structures, machines, and systems. In fact, the development of electronic trading platforms and algorithmic trading strategies can be compared to the creation of complex engineering systems.

COMPUTING

The financial markets are closely linked to the rapid growth of computing technology. High-speed computing systems have revolutionized the way financial markets operate, and the use of algorithms to execute trades, analyse data, and monitor market trends has become a fundamental part of trading and investing.

CONCLUSION

The financial markets are a complex system formed by the confluence of various forces. The interaction between these factors can be unpredictable, leading to sudden and unexpected market behaviour. As investors and traders, it is crucial to be aware of these factors and assess the potential impact they could have on investments. I recommend creating rules and sticking to them to try to avoid excessive risk. A thorough understanding of the technical, fundamental, and external factors that shape market behaviour can lead to improved decision-making, which is crucial for success in trading and investing in the financial markets.

CHAPTER 2

Key Components of Confluences

CONFLUENCE IS MORE than the sum of its parts. Each factor, indicator, and data point provides specific information, but it's not until these single elements blend and combine that a whole, clear picture emerges.

I didn't start out with this understanding. As I mentioned earlier, I first began trading in the late nineties. I started by trading currencies on the foreign exchange (forex) market because they could be traded any time of day or night. In the beginning, I spent a great deal of time reading the forex charts, but it was a lot of information to keep up with on a daily basis. That led to longer-term swing trading of forex and eventually swing trading stocks. This was better for me because it involved less risk and also moved at a much slower trading pace, which was especially beneficial since I was working full-time in the army and trading in my spare time.

Back then, it was a different world. Technology was improving, but most data analysis still involved a lot of time and hard work. I was learning as much as I could as quickly as I could. I collected massive amounts of data (statistics, charts, anything I could find). I researched, reviewed, and started over again.

I searched for better ways to do things, but the more I traded, the more questions I had. Should I keep or sell a stock? Is this the right trade? When should I enter and exit trades? I spent countless hours looking at individual pieces of data until they suddenly started to merge together and make sense. The individual components started to become part of a larger, cohesive whole. I was excited to discover that the combined and layered information provided meaningful signals that gave me better answers to my questions. It was the beginning of my confluence strategy.

After working out this strategy, I needed to optimize how I compiled all the data. By the early "noughties" (or 2000s for the non-Brits), software solutions were advancing, though they weren't quite up to the task of tracking all the key components that fed the confluence strategy I was building. I couldn't quite migrate to a day trading strategy, but I was making progress. Swing trading was helping me hone my skills and spot patterns of behaviour and confluences.

It wasn't until 2013 that technology was advanced enough to help streamline my trading process. I wanted to speed things up and create tools that could combine massive amounts of information to identify patterns of confluence.

Technology also allowed me to reach my personal goal of transferring my knowledge and skills to day trading, which, compared to swing trading, requires much quicker analysis and sometimes split-second decisions. My next journey was beginning — to develop software that kept in mind how the behaviour of confluences developed from combining key components.

In this chapter, I want to examine the key components that make up confluence. I'll start by discussing the ones I use the most. Individually, these factors provide useful information, but combined, they can create a strong, cohesive picture of patterns and signal-specific behaviour.

The key components that make up confluences are diverse, but the categories that I generally take into consideration include:

- Technical analysis
- Fundamental factors
- Sentiment analysis
- Timeframes
- Trading volume
- Correlations

Each component provides a different perspective on the market and helps develop an effective confluence strategy.

TECHNICAL ANALYSIS

Technical analysis tools are used by traders to identify potential market movements. Specifically, traders analyse past market data and use those findings to make trading decisions and predict future trends — important information to consider as part of a confluence strategy. A few commonly used technical indicators include moving averages, support and resistance levels, and price action patterns.

Many useful technical analysis tools exist, but I'd like to focus on an important technological advancement that has simplified and automated technical analysis — algorithms.

In the past, technical analysis required a deep understanding of mathematical and statistical models as well as the ability to interpret and analyse complex data sets. This often required a high degree of expertise and experience and could be prohibitively time-consuming and costly for many traders and investors.

However, as financial markets evolved, so, too, did the methods used by traders and investors to analyse and make decisions. Advances in technology and computing power meant that complex technical analysis measurements and calculations could now easily be accomplished with algorithms, which can process vast amounts of data and perform complex analyses in a matter of seconds — providing traders and investors with real-time information and insights that can help them make more profitable decisions.

AUTOMATED TRADING

Algorithmic trading has made it possible for traders and investors to automate many of their trading activities, reducing the need for manual interventions and allowing them to take advantage of opportunities that would otherwise be missed. This has helped to level the playing field and has made trading and investing more accessible to a wider range of individuals and institutions.

When it comes to trading and investing in the financial markets, it is important to understand that automated trading strategies are not a one-size-fits-all solution. Even experienced traders who use automation software should not expect any system to be a fire-and-forget solution.

Why is this the case? It's simple — market conditions and confluences are constantly changing. This means that any automated trading strategy must be re-optimized frequently to remain effective in the face of changing conditions. Unfortunately, there is currently no true AI capable of spotting these changes and updating strategies automatically.

Algorithms may be able to follow a set of rules, but they cannot think for themselves or adapt to changing situations on their own. This is something that every trader needs to understand when utilizing automated trading strategies. Simply setting your strategy and walking away is not enough. You must be willing to monitor and adjust your strategy as needed in order to achieve ongoing success.

Algorithmic technology is incorporated, to some degree, in all trading software and can be used to streamline and simplify even the most complex strategies. However, it's important to remember that it is not AI and cannot independently think or make decisions. It's a useful (perhaps even essential) tool, but it requires monitoring. Think of it as one of many tools to be used as part of an effective technical analysis.

TECHNOLOGY TO IDENTIFY CONFLUENCES

Harmonic Pattern Theory is a sophisticated method of technical analysis that involves traders conducting numerous technical Fibonacci measurements to identify confluences and accurately predict market trends. This strategy is a time-consuming and complicated process that involves the measurement of Fibonacci extensions and retracements to determine areas where the pattern should complete. It is particularly challenging for day traders who cannot complete the process in short timeframes.

A Harmonic Pattern comprises four pivots: A, B, C, and D. These pivots form the basis for identifying and analysing market trends. By studying the sequence and proportionality of these pivots, traders can gain insights into potential market reversals and predict future price movements. Understanding and utilizing Harmonic Patterns can be a valuable tool in technical analysis, allowing traders to make informed decisions and take advantage of market opportunities.

Algorithms can be utilized to make these calculations quickly and reliably and can provide the ability to identify the high-probability zones for any type of harmonic pattern to complete. It is this completion zone that traders are interested in. If a Harmonic Pattern completes its D pivot in this zone of complex Fibonacci confluences, then the resulting trade is high probability.

TAKEAWAYS

The key to trading and investing in the financial markets is to remain knowledgeable and adaptable. Keep an eye on market conditions and be prepared to adjust your strategy as needed to stay ahead of the curve. With the right approach, an automated trading system can be an incredibly valuable tool, but it should never be relied on as a fool-proof solution.

The evolution of technology and computing power has had a profound impact on trading and investing in the financial markets. With algorithms that are able to accomplish tasks that were previously considered complex and time-consuming, traders and investors can now make more informed decisions, capitalize on trends, and drive greater profits.

FUNDAMENTAL ANALYSIS

Fundamental analysis is another key component to consider as part of confluence. It examines macroeconomic and financial indicators to help traders evaluate the value of stocks or securities. By looking at fundamental factors, traders get an idea of how these elements can impact market movements. Other fundamental factors include economic conditions, industry trends, gross domestic product (GDP) growth, inflation, interest rates, and company earnings.

While a plethora of factors can impact financial market movements, investors use fundamental factors to gauge the health and performance of an economy. Understanding these indicators and how they relate to market movements can be the key to successful trading and investing in the financial markets.

I consider the following factors particularly helpful to consider as part of a fundamental analysis.

MACROECONOMIC INDICATORS

GDP growth is one of the most important macroeconomic indicators to consider. This number reflects the rate at which a country's economy is growing. GDP growth is often seen as a measure of the overall health of an economy and can have a significant impact on market movements. When GDP growth is high, investors tend to be more optimistic about the market, and stocks and other assets tend to perform well. Conversely, when GDP growth slows down or contracts, investors become more cautious, and markets tend to experience declines.

Inflation is another key macroeconomic indicator, providing information on the rate at which prices are rising in an economy. Inflation can have a significant impact on market movements, as it can affect the value of currencies and the cost of goods and services. When inflation is high, investors tend to be more cautious and may shift their investments to assets that are less likely to be impacted by inflation, such as real estate, commodities, or stocks. Conversely, when inflation is low, investors may become more optimistic and may be more willing to take on riskier investments.

FINANCIAL INDICATORS

Interest rates are an important financial indicator that can impact market movements. When interest rates are low, many investors may be more willing to borrow money to invest in the market, as borrowing costs are lower. This can lead to increased demand for assets like stocks and other securities, which can cause prices to rise. Conversely, when interest rates are high, investors may be less willing to borrow money, which can lead to decreased demand for assets and lower market prices.

Company earnings are perhaps one of the most important financial indicators for investors. Profitability is ultimately the driver of a company's stock price, and if earnings are strong, investors tend to become more bullish on a particular stock or sector. Conversely, weak earnings can lead to lower stock prices and decreased demand for a particular type of security. Watching corporate earnings reports can be a powerful tool for investors looking to make smart trading decisions and capitalize on market trends.

TAKEAWAYS

It is important to note that macroeconomic and financial indicators do not exist in a vacuum. They interact with one another in complex ways. Understanding the confluence of these various indicators can help investors understand how they can impact market movements.

For example, a combination of high GDP growth, low inflation, and low interest rates may create a market environment that is ripe for bullish activity, while a combination of high inflation, high interest rates, and declining corporate earnings may signal a bearish market.

It's essential for traders and investors in the financial markets to recognise the importance of the relationship between macroeconomic and financial indicators and market movements. Understanding these indicators and how they interact can provide valuable insights into market trends and effective trading strategies. By paying close attention to factors like GDP growth, inflation, interest rates, and company earnings, investors can make smarter investment decisions and capitalize on market opportunities.

SENTIMENT ANALYSIS

Sentiment analysis is the next component to consider. It evaluates how market sentiment and emotional biases can impact price movements. Using this technique, traders collect data from a variety of sources (news releases, social media sentiment, and investor sentiment surveys, to name a few) and use that information to make better-informed decisions.

Simply put, market sentiment is defined as the overall attitude of market participants towards a particular asset or the market as a whole. It is the collective perception of investors and traders about future market expectations that influences market prices.

Emotional biases refer to the mental shortcuts and irrational beliefs that investors use to make decisions. These biases can be based on past experiences, cultural beliefs, and cognitive biases that limit an investor's ability to make rational decisions. Emotional biases can lead to excessive optimism or pessimism, which can result in irrational buying or selling.

A variety of information sources can be used to assess market sentiment, including:

- **News releases** — provide details (like economic data, corporate earnings, and political developments) that can have a significant impact on market sentiment. Positive news can lead to an increase in demand for the asset, while negative news can lead to decreased supply and lower demand.
- **Social media sentiment analysis** — recognizes that social media is a global tool for communication and information sharing. Millions of users are actively posting their opinions on various issues. Collecting and analysing this information

allows traders and investors to gauge market expectations and identify potential trends or shifts in the market.

- **Investor sentiment surveys** — measure investor's attitudes and expectations about the future price movements of an asset or market. They are designed to capture the bullish or bearish sentiment of investors. A bullish sentiment indicates positive market expectations, while a bearish sentiment indicates negative market expectations.

A confluence of these factors is extremely valuable in accurately predicting future price movements. A combination of positive news releases, social media sentiment, and bullish investor sentiment surveys can lead to an increase in market demand, which results in higher prices. On the contrary, a combination of negative news, social media sentiment, and bearish investor sentiment surveys can lead to a decrease in demand, resulting in lower prices.

Other factors that may impact a sentiment analysis include:

- **Unusual options activity.** Options trading allows traders to bet on the future movements of an asset's price. Unusual options activity occurs when there is a significantly higher than average trading volume, which may indicate a potential shift in market sentiment. It is worth noting that unusual options activity should not be used as the sole basis for making trading decisions but should be considered alongside other factors such as news releases, social media sentiment, and investor sentiment surveys.

- **Buying and selling of shares** by insiders who own certain percentages of the company and are in the management team. This information is publicly available and can affect market sentiment in various ways. For example, if insiders are buying shares, it can indicate that they have confidence in the company's future performance, and this could lead to an increase in market demand, which will result in higher stock prices.

TAKEAWAYS

Market sentiment and emotional biases are key factors in driving price movements in financial markets. As a trader or investor, it's important to consider a variety of factors when analysing market sentiment, such as monitoring news releases, tracking social media sentiment, conducting investor sentiment surveys, examining unusual options activity, and keeping track of insider buying and selling.

By analysing these factors, traders and investors can more accurately predict market sentiment and make informed decisions to better position themselves in the market. However, it's important to note that market sentiment is not an exact science. It's a combination of probabilities and likelihoods. As such, successful traders and investors exercise caution and discipline when making trading decisions based on sentiment analysis.

Fortunately, advances in technology have made it possible to analyse and correlate these factors more effectively. The xBrat Stocks Predator, for example, is a powerful tool that can help traders and investors identify market trends and make more informed decisions based on real-time data. By leveraging technology to analyse market sentiment, traders and investors can stay ahead of the game and make more profitable trades.

TIMEFRAMES

Traders are always looking for ways to gain an edge and make better decisions that lead to profits. Among the main factors that can affect a trader's analysis and decision-making process are the different timeframes they are analysing — an important component to consider when creating an effective confluence strategy. Put simply, a timeframe refers to how long a trend is expected to last in the market, but it can have a big impact on a trader's analysis and decision-making process. For example, a trader may consider a longer-term trend on a weekly chart while looking for a short-term entry on the daily or hourly chart.

Timeframes can range from minutes to months and even years, and each can give different insights into the market and its trends. For example, a trader may use a longer-term timeframe, such as the weekly chart, to identify the overall trend of a particular stock. This can provide a bigger picture of the market and help traders identify key levels of support and resistance.

On the other hand, traders may also use shorter-term timeframes, such as daily or hourly charts, to identify potential entry and exit points for trades. By analysing these shorter-term periods, traders can identify smaller patterns and trends that may not be apparent on longer-term charts.

TAKEAWAYS

Trading information is available for a wide variety of timeframes. It's important to note that each timeframe has its own strengths and weaknesses. Traders need to carefully analyse and understand what type of information each one provides before making any trading decisions.

It's crucial for traders to carefully analyse the information provided by each timeframe to understand the strengths and weaknesses of each in order to make informed trading decisions based on the insights gleaned from this analysis. For example, a trader looking to make quick profits may focus primarily on short-term data that indicates potential rapid fluctuations in a financial instrument's price. Without examining longer timeframes, they may fail to recognize broader trends, missing crucial information that could inform long-term investment decisions.

CHART TYPES

Let's take a closer look at some of the different chart types that traders can use to analyse factors that impact the financial markets. Traders use these every day, so it's good to have a solid understanding of how to use them.

Line Charts
Line charts are one of the simplest and most commonly used chart types in trading. They are created by connecting the closing prices of a financial instrument over a certain period of time. Line charts are great for identifying trends and key levels of support and resistance but may not be effective in identifying smaller price movements.

Bar Charts
Bar charts provide more information than line charts as they also include the high, low, and opening prices of a financial instrument in addition to the closing prices. Bar charts can be a great way to identify price ranges and price momentum, but they can also, at times, be difficult to read.

Candlestick Charts
Candlestick charts are one of the most popular chart types used by traders. They provide a lot of information about price action, including the opening and closing prices, highs, and lows. Candlestick charts can also be a great way to identify patterns and trends, making them a powerful tool for traders.

UniRenko Charts
Unlike traditional charts, UniRenko charts are based on a unique method of plotting data. This chart type takes into account the price fluctuations in the market, and with every movement of a specified tick value, a new bar is created.

The main advantage of using UniRenko charts is that they filter out market noise and prevent traders from getting distracted by insignificant price fluctuations. This allows traders to focus on significant movements and make informed trading decisions based on these movements.

TRADING VOLUME

Trading volume refers to the total number of shares or contracts that have been traded during a given period of time. Tracking trading volume reveals investor interest in particular companies as well as more general momentum (up or down) in stocks, sectors, or assets. Following the amount of trading activity can provide insight into market sentiment and potential price movements, as it reflects the level of demand for a particular financial instrument.

PRICE AND SENTIMENT

Trading volume can signal when price changes might occur. Traders track this pricing information using accumulation and distribution candles. An accumulation candle occurs when traders accumulate more shares at the ask (via buy orders) than at the bid (via sell orders) within a single candle. To qualify as an accumulation candle, it must not only close higher overall but also have a higher volume compared to the preceding candle. These accumulation candles can be for any timeframe that a trader is monitoring. If a financial instrument experiences two or more consecutive accumulation candles, it indicates strength or a bullish trend (remember, the volume of the second accumulation candle needs to be higher than the previous one, showcasing a steady increase in volume during a trending wave).

On the other hand, a distribution candle represents the dispersion or selling of shares. It is crucial to note that distribution candles are associated with selling, not buying (which is accumulation). The key aspect in identifying a distribution candle is that the overall price must close lower, accompanied by a higher volume compared to the preceding candle. If a financial instrument exhibits two or more consecutive distribution candles, it suggests weakness or a bearish trend (again, the volume of the second distribution candle has to be higher than the previous volume).

I've developed a Volume Behaviour Indicator that can help traders interpret trade volume and have included it with the purchase of this book. The Indicator identifies candles and changes their colour according to whether the volume for that time period is an accumulation or distribution candle or if it has less volume than that of the previous candle. This can help users make better and smarter real-time decisions. By understanding accumulation and distribution candles, traders can gain valuable insights into market trends.

Measuring average volume can also help gauge market sentiment. By calculating the average volume

over a given period of time, traders and investors can get a sense of the level of interest in a particular financial instrument. Higher-than-average volume can indicate that a particular financial instrument is in demand, while lower-than-average volume can indicate that there is less interest.

Traders and investors can also use volume to confirm the validity of price movements. For example, if prices are rising on high volume, this can indicate that there is strong buying pressure, which could be a signal to buy. Conversely, if prices are rising on low volume, this can indicate that the price movement is not sustainable, and a reversal may be imminent.

In addition to measuring average volume, traders and investors can also look for confluences between volume and price action. For example, if prices are making slightly higher highs and higher lows, but volume is decreasing, this can be a sign of weakness. It indicates that there is less demand for the financial instrument. Even though prices are still rising, this may be a signal to sell, as the price movement may not be sustainable. Conversely, if prices are making slightly lower lows and lower highs, but volume is increasing, this can be a sign of strength. It indicates that there is increasing demand for the financial instrument, even though prices are still falling. This can be a signal to buy, as the price movement may not be sustainable.

TAKEAWAYS

Trading volume is an important signal that traders and investors can use to gain insight into market sentiment and potential price movements. By using accumulation and distribution candles, measuring average volume, and looking for confluences between volume and price action, traders and investors can better assess the demand for a particular financial instrument and make more informed trading decisions.

CORRELATIONS

It can be overwhelming for traders and investors to try to gain intimate knowledge of every single asset that is trading on all the different markets across the globe. However, we can stay aware of the correlations between these assets in order to properly gauge their normal and abnormal behaviours.

By understanding relationships and interdependencies between different assets, we can identify patterns and movements within the market that may be indicative of shifts or trends across multiple sectors. For example, if we notice a sudden drop in the stock prices of oil companies, this may be correlated with an increase in the price of gold as investors seek out alternative safe havens.

TRADING AND CORRELATIONS

When day trading, it is crucial to have a set of reliable correlations upon which to base your trading decisions. I personally use a correlation set that includes the four major indexes in the United States — the S&P500, Nasdaq, Dow Jones, and the Russell. However, it is not enough for these indexes to simply be moving. They must also be in a state of confluence, which means they are all trending in the same direction.

In my experience, if there is any sector rotation from any of these indexes (indicating that one of them is losing value while the others are gaining), then I become wary of any potential futures trades at that moment. A lack of correlation amongst these four major indexes can lead to confusion and a lack of clear direction, which can ultimately lead to unfavourable trading outcomes.

Therefore, as a prudent day trader, I wait patiently for all four indexes to align before making any decisions. By waiting until there is a clear direction of movement amongst these major indexes, I can be more confident in my trades and other correlations to avoid any unnecessary risks. Ultimately, the key to successful day trading involves basing your decisions on sound correlations and remaining patient until all indicators are in agreement.

US DOLLAR

The US dollar (USD) plays a pivotal role in shaping market dynamics. This is primarily because some of the highest value stocks in the world are listed in the United States, and the majority of global commodities, such as oil and gold, are priced in USD. This makes it an excellent way to understand the relationship between different assets and market correlations. Additionally, the USD serves as a benchmark against which all other currencies are evaluated. As such, it is common for various currencies to be pegged against the USD, making it the world's reserve currency.

These factors create a situation where any fluctuations in the USD's value can significantly impact other asset classes and their correlations. In other words, when the USD moves up or down, normal market conditions tend to change, and the effects ripple across various markets, creating a confluence of correlations. The intricate relationship between the USD and other asset classes is something that every trader and investor must understand to make informed decisions.

I've created a graphic (Image 2.1) to illustrate main market correlations and the US Dollar Index ($DXY). The $DXY measures the value of the USD against other currencies. If the $DXY moves up in value, so too does oil, but Euro and gold prices go down. Whilst the S&P500 index usually follows the USD up, bonds have an inverse correlation and move down. On the left of $DXY, the opposite correlations are true. Any changes to the value of the USD can have far-reaching effects on other asset classes. Therefore, keeping a close eye on the USD's movements remains essential for any trader seeking to succeed in the markets.

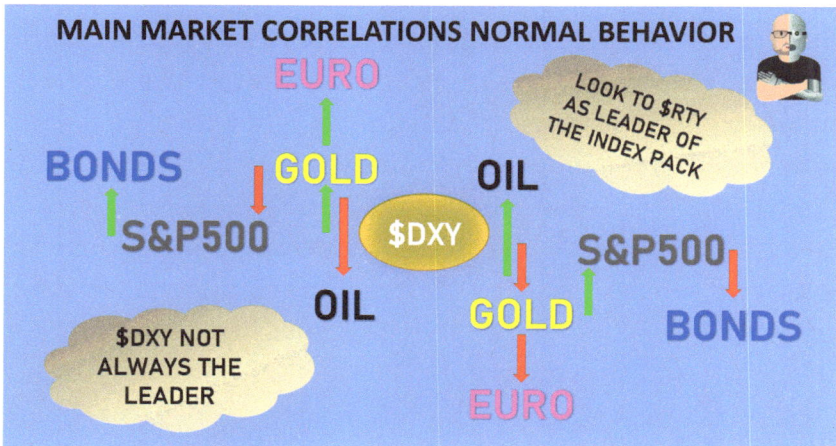

Image 2.1 – Fluctuations in the USD's Value Can Significantly Impact Other Asset Classes and Their Correlations.

TAKEAWAYS

Having an awareness of correlations allows us to better anticipate market movements and make informed investment decisions. We can use this knowledge to diversify our portfolios and mitigate risk by investing in assets that have a low or negative correlation with our existing holdings.

A strong understanding of market correlations can help us find reasons for abnormal behaviour and navigate the complex and dynamic landscape of the financial markets with greater confidence and precision.

CONCLUSION

Overall, confluence is a cornerstone of successful trading, as it requires the integration of many important components. By blending technical and fundamental analysis with sentiment trends, chart timeframes, trading volume, and correlations, traders can develop informed trading strategies. By utilizing these insights, traders can enhance their profitability and develop a more comprehensive and effective trading plan that is both founded on sound principles and anchored to an understanding of market **behaviour**. As we move towards an increasingly data-driven market, knowledge about these key components and their interactions becomes more crucial to traders' success.

SECTION 2

CATALYSTS AND CONFLUENCES

CHAPTER 3

Catalysts and Confluences

I THINK OF catalysts as sparks that incite market activity. More specifically, they are events, like company news or economic data, that positively or negatively impact the price action of a stock or financial instrument. When trading, catalysts are driving forces behind a security's movement, which makes them essential to understand. Recognizing how catalysts operate as sparks that enhance or break down confluences is crucial to your success

Confluence involves collecting and analysing different factors, indicators, or signals. How these elements come together can suggest a potential trend or movement in the markets. In this scenario, a catalyst acts as a disruptor and pushes confluence in a reactive way. Put simply, one decision or event can be a catalyst that leads to a confluence of other events. I experienced this first-hand during my active military years.

I was an engineering manager with the 1st Regiment Royal Horse Artillery. We were in Canada at the British

Army Training Unit Suffield (BATUS) for a full-scale battle-group live-firing exercise. I was responsible for overseeing engineering support and logistics for the entire operation.

To prepare, I met with the battery commander leading the exercise, and he expressed his desire to incorporate all six AS90 self-propelled howitzers into the exercise, though previous battlegroup exercises had typically utilized only four.

While two additional artillery pieces may not seem like a significant change, it had an astounding impact on the logistical planning required to support the exercise, necessitating additional support vehicles. While the addition of these vehicles might seem to be a minor detail, it added immense complexity to the planning process and escalated the risks associated with the operation.

Furthermore, this increase created a catalyst that had the potential to break down the support that we could offer. My complement of engineers remained at the same level, and no increase was made to the number of support vehicles available. The flow of the entire battlegroup operation was highly susceptible to breakdown, and if that happened, I would need to call on Battle Group Assets for additional support. Overall, this seemingly minor addition represented a monumental logistical challenge that had to be carefully navigated and managed to ensure a successful operation.

I requested additional support before the operation began but didn't receive any. Then, my fears became reality. My one and only recovery asset was towing an AS90 to the next firing position when another AS90 broke down. Not only that, three of the support vehicles carrying the artillery ammunition got "bogged in" — stuck in mud.

This confluence of unfortunate events meant only four guns were available for the fire mission, and battlegroup operations had to be slowed down whilst assets from other units were tasked with helping both the stuck vehicles carrying ammunition and the broken-down AS90. It took six hours to get everything going again. On the upside, I had an additional recovery asset and a crew of engineers permanently added to my support vehicles for the remainder of the operation.

In this situation, the confluence of events that broke down the flow of operations can be traced back to the decision (or catalyst) to add two artillery pieces. People much higher up than me would learn valuable lessons from this choice and the ensuing events. You would think changes might be made to prevent such confluences from breaking down operations in the future, but if you're ex-military, you can probably guess whether they did this or simply waited until it happened again to react!

In any case, it's important for traders and investors to understand and learn to identify catalysts. I'll review some of the most impactful catalysts that can enhance or break down confluences in the financial markets, specifically economic data releases, geopolitical events, corporate earnings reports, central bank decisions, and technical analysis indicators. What follows is a discussion of these types of catalysts.

ECONOMIC DATA RELEASES

Key economic indicators, such as interest rates, GDP growth, employment figures, and inflation rates, can significantly impact market sentiment and prices. Positive economic data can enhance a confluence, while negative data can break it down.

Economic data releases help traders and investors understand the direction and strength of the market. Specific economic indicators, such as interest rates, GDP growth, employment figures, and inflation rates, can significantly influence traders' sentiment and prices.

When trading, it is essential to keep an eye on upcoming economic data releases, as they can be potential catalysts for price movements and can confirm a confluence in other areas. For example, before the release of a major report, there is often an increase in market volatility. Therefore, traders should only trade when there is sufficient leverage to meet their goals and consider the risks of holding a position through major economic data releases.

Staying informed about economic trends is one way to make well-informed trading decisions based on a strong analysis of current and potential market direction. Examples of economic data releases impacting financial market confluences are plentiful, as these events often cause significant fluctuations in the values of various securities and assets.

One such example is the release of US nonfarm payroll data, which is released on the first Friday of every month and provides information on the employment situation in the country. When the data reveals a higher number of jobs was added than expected, it typically results in a rally in US equities, as investors view the news as a sign of economic growth and bullish sentiment. Conversely, a lower-than-expected number leads to a sell-off, as investors take it as a bearish signal for the US economy.

Another example is the release of inflation data, particularly the consumer price index (CPI), which measures the price changes of a basket of goods and services over time. When the

CPI comes in above expectations, it typically causes a sell-off in US government bonds, as investors anticipate a rise in interest rates to combat inflation. This also has a negative impact on stocks, as higher interest rates make it more expensive for companies to borrow money, which tends to decrease earning potential and slow down economic growth.

Finally, the release of gross domestic product (GDP) data, which measures the value of all goods and services produced within a country over a certain period of time, has a significant impact on the financial markets. An unexpectedly high GDP print typically results in a rally in equities, as investors view it as a sign of strong economic growth. Conversely, a shockingly low GDP number triggers a sell-off and typically leads to a flight to safety in assets such as bonds and gold as investors try to hedge against an impending recession.

TAKEAWAYS

Financial market confluences are often shaped by economic data releases, which can cause significant fluctuations in the values of various securities and assets. As a trader or investor, keeping an eye on these events and their potential impact is key to making informed decisions and maximizing profits in the financial markets.

GEOPOLITICAL EVENTS

Geopolitical events have always been an influential element in trading and investing in the financial markets. The outcome of such events can either enhance or break down a confluence in the markets. As global politics evolves, the consequences of events such as trade tensions, geopolitical conflicts, and elections can trigger dramatic changes in market sentiments and create significant volatility in the market.

There is no better example of how geopolitical events can impact financial markets than the 2014 Russian invasion and annexation of Ukraine's Crimean Peninsula. The conflict sent shockwaves through global stock markets and caused the price of gold to soar. With anxiety about the potential impact the escalating crisis could have on world economies, investors rushed to buy gold as a hedge against geopolitical risks.

The consequences of this invasion played out well into 2022. Even though the world slowly adjusted to the new reality following the conflict, the standoff triggered by this event had ongoing repercussions in the global financial markets. The tension between Russia and the West resulted in sanctions that slowed economic growth in many regions for many years, highlighting how major political events can shape economic outcomes and market conditions over an extended period.

Another example of geopolitical events impacting market sentiment is the massive spike in oil prices that occurred in 2010. During the Arab Spring, political unrest and social turmoil triggered a sharp rise in oil prices. Because oil prices directly impact nearly every sector of the economy, any significant rise in prices often has an equally significant knock-on effect on other financial markets. When oil prices spike, investors may anticipate the impact of such rises on the economy, and this can result in significant market movements.

Indeed, as a result of this upheaval in the Middle East, stock market indexes reacted with volatility, dropping sharply in some instances. The uncertainty surrounding the situation, compounded by the lack of immediate resolution, continued to affect market sentiment for months, causing challenges for businesses that relied on oil and prompting investors to adopt a cautious approach.

Across industries, no market is immune to the uncertainties and risks created by geopolitical events. From the escalating US-China trade war to political instabilities in different parts of the world, shifting political events can cause significant economic transitions that have lasting effects and can result in severe financial losses for businesses that are unable to adapt.

TAKEAWAYS

It is essential for investors to appreciate how significant global politics can be in the financial markets. Market sentiment can be highly volatile during critical events and shocks, making it challenging to predict the most appropriate trading or investment strategies. However, by staying up to date with geopolitical developments and remaining informed about global economies, investors can adopt more nuanced and effective approaches to investing or trading, thereby protecting their portfolios and ensuring long-term investment success.

CORPORATE EARNINGS REPORTS

Corporate earnings reports are important indicators of the financial health of individual companies, as well as the state of the overall economy. Strong earnings reports can enhance a confluence, while weak reports can break a confluence down.

In the case of large companies with high market capitalizations, the release of earnings reports can often have a significant impact on the stock market. The S&P500 is a stock market index that tracks the performance of 500 large companies listed on stock exchanges in the United States. These companies are selected for inclusion in the index based on various factors, including market capitalization, liquidity, and industry sector representation. When these companies announce better-than-expected earnings, their share price is likely to rise, which can have a substantial impact on the performance of the S&P500 as a whole.

As of May 2021, the five largest companies on the index were Apple Inc., Microsoft Corporation, Amazon.com Inc., Facebook Inc., and Tesla Inc. These five companies alone accounted for over 22 percent of the total market capitalization of the index. Their earnings reports can affect the index and, through market correlations, disturb or enhance confluences across other sectors and markets.

Conversely, if a company reports weak earnings, its share price is likely to fall, possibly dragging down the performance of the index with it. This phenomenon can be particularly pronounced in the case of large companies with high market capitalizations, as their movements can have an outsized impact on the index.

In addition to the impact on the S&P500 index, the earnings reports of large companies can also have wider spillover effects on other sectors and markets. For example, if a major technology company such as Apple or Microsoft reports strong earnings, this could potentially boost the performance of the entire technology sector as well as other related sectors, such as consumer electronics or telecommunications. Similarly, a weak earnings report from a major oil and gas company like ExxonMobil could potentially drag down the performance of the energy sector and related markets, such as commodities and currencies.

Another way in which corporate earnings reports can impact the stock market is through market correlations. Market correlation refers to the degree to which the movements of different stocks or markets are aligned with one another. In periods of high correlation, many different stocks and markets may move in the same direction based on similar underlying factors.

In the case of earnings reports, high market correlation can be particularly important as it can amplify the spillover effects of individual company earnings across different sectors and markets. For example, if a major retailer such as Walmart or Target reports strong earnings, it can have a positive impact not only on other retailers but also on consumer goods companies, transportation and logistics companies, and even the broader market as a whole. This is because strong earnings from a major retailer suggest that consumer demand is high, and the economy may be overall healthy.

On the other hand, if a major retailer reports weak earnings, it can trigger a sell-off across the entire sector and beyond. This is because weak earnings suggest that consumer demand may be low, and the economy may be struggling. Furthermore, these sectors may be correlated with other markets, such as currencies or commodities, which could also experience spillover effects from the earnings report.

Apple Inc's earnings reports have a significant impact on the US stock market, signalling to investors the overall health of the economy and the performance of companies within the technology industry. When Apple releases its financial earnings reports, it often creates a ripple effect across the US stock markets. This is mainly because Apple is one of the most valuable companies in the world, with a market capitalization of over $2 trillion, making it one of the most heavily traded stocks.

For instance, in the first quarter of 2021, Apple reported net sales of $89.6 billion with a net income of $23.6 billion, a figure that surpassed analysts' expectations. In response to this announcement, the stock price of Apple increased by 3 percent within a few hours of the financial announcement. This increase also had a positive effect on the overall US stock market, with the NASDAQ and S&P 500 also increasing in value.

In addition to its potential effect on the financial markets in general, Apple's earnings also impact the US dollar because of its impact on the overall economy. Apple is the largest company in the world by market capitalization and one of the largest taxpayers in the United States. As a result, a positive earnings report can strengthen the dollar as investors become more bullish on the economy, resulting in increased demand for the currency. Conversely, a negative report can weaken the dollar as investors lose confidence. When investors become more hesitant about the state of the economy, they may sell off their investments, leading to a decrease in demand for the US dollar and potentially reducing its value against other currencies.

TAKEAWAYS

Corporate earnings reports are important indicators of the financial health of individual companies and the state of the overall economy. The spillover effects of these earnings reports can be amplified through market correlations, potentially causing disturbances or enhancing confluences across different sectors and markets. As traders and investors, paying close attention to corporate earnings reports and understanding their potential impact on the wider stock market and economy can make the difference between making a successful investment or experiencing a loss.

CENTRAL BANK DECISIONS

The decisions made by central banks, such as the Federal Reserve or the European Central Bank, can have a profound impact on the financial markets, particularly when it comes to interest rates and market liquidity. Their policies can either enhance or break down a confluence in the market. As a trader or investor in the financial markets, it is vital to understand the role of central banks in shaping the market as well as the factors that influence their policy decisions.

One of the primary functions of central banks is to control inflation and maintain the stability of their respective economies. To achieve that, central banks use various monetary policy tools such as interest rate adjustments, open market operations, and reserve requirements.

Interest rate adjustments are perhaps the most common and effective tool used by central banks. By raising or lowering interest rates, central banks can influence borrowing costs for businesses and consumers. Higher interest rates encourage savings and reduce the demand for loans, while lower interest rates stimulate borrowing and spending.

For example, in the United States, the Federal Reserve sets the target federal funds rate, which is the rate at which banks lend money to each other overnight. This rate indirectly affects many other interest rates in the economy, including mortgage rates, credit card rates, and auto loan rates. When the Federal Reserve lowers interest rates, borrowing costs decline, which spurs consumer spending and business investment. The opposite effect is seen when the Federal Reserve raises interest rates, as borrowing becomes more expensive, which can curb spending and investment.

Central banks also use open market operations to influence market liquidity, which refers to the amount of money available for borrowing and lending. In an open market operation, the central bank buys or sells government securities, which affects the amount of money in circulation. When the central bank buys government securities, it injects money into the banking system, which increases market liquidity. Conversely, when the central bank sells securities, it reduces the amount of money in circulation, which decreases liquidity.

In addition to interest rate adjustments and open market operations, central banks may also use reserve requirements to influence lending activity. Reserve requirements are the amount of money that banks must hold in reserve to cover their deposits. By raising reserve requirements, central banks decrease the amount of money available for lending, which can limit borrowing and lower inflation. By lowering reserve requirements, central banks can make more money available for lending, which can stimulate economic growth.

Central bank decisions can have both short-term and long-term effects on the financial markets. For example, a surprise interest rate cut can lead to a stock market rally as investors anticipate higher profits for businesses due to lower borrowing costs. On the other hand, a sudden interest rate hike can lead to a sell-off as investors worry about the impact on corporate profits and the economy as a whole. Central bank decisions can also affect exchange rates, as higher interest rates tend to strengthen a country's currency, while lower rates can weaken it.

In recent years, central banks around the world have implemented unconventional monetary policies, such as quantitative easing, to stimulate their economies in the wake of the global financial crisis. Quantitative easing involves the central bank purchasing large quantities of government securities or other assets to inject money into the economy. The goal is to increase market liquidity and encourage lending and investment. While quantitative easing has been successful in jump-starting economic growth in various countries, it has also raised concerns about inflation and asset price bubbles.

TAKEAWAYS

Central bank decisions are critical to understanding and predicting the behaviour of financial markets. As a trader or investor, it is essential to keep an eye on central bank policies and announcements, as they can have far-reaching effects on interest rates, exchange rates, and liquidity. By staying up to date on central bank decisions and understanding the factors that influence them, traders and investors can make smarter and more informed trading decisions.

TECHNICAL ANALYSIS INDICATORS

As previously discussed, technical analysis involves analysing charts and price patterns to identify trends and predict potential market movements. Although it is not a foolproof method, it provides valuable insights to market participants. Indicators such as moving averages, Bollinger Bands, and the relative strength index (RSI) can enhance or break down a confluence, depending on their signals.

MOVING AVERAGES

Moving averages are one of the most frequently used technical indicators in the financial markets. A moving average is a simple calculation of the average price over a certain number of periods. It is used to smooth out price fluctuations and show the general market direction. As the name suggests, it is an indicator that lags behind the price action in the market. This means that it provides information based on past price movements rather than predicting future price movements. Consequently, it is important to complement it with other indicators for a more robust analysis.

BOLLINGER BANDS

Bollinger Bands consist of three bands — an upper band, a lower band, and a simple moving average (SMA) in between. The upper and lower bands are calculated by adding and subtracting a multiple of the standard deviation from the SMA. They are used to measure the volatility of a market and identify potential breakouts or pullbacks. When the price breaks above the upper band, it is considered overbought, and when it breaks below the lower band, it is considered oversold.

RELATIVE STRENGTH INDEX (RSI)

RSI is a momentum indicator that measures the speed and change of price movements. It oscillates between 0 and 100, with a reading above 70 indicating overbought conditions and a reading below 30 indicating oversold conditions. It is used to identify potential trend reversals and market fluctuations.

It is important to note that these indicators are just tools and should not be used in isolation. It is crucial to complement them with fundamental analysis, market sentiment, and other relevant information before making any trading or investment decisions.

Institutional traders are known to use technical indicators extensively, and their interpretation of these indicators is what can move markets. They use these indicators to identify trading opportunities, manage their risks, and maximize their returns. However, as retail traders, it is important to understand that they have access to more resources and information than we do. Hence, it is crucial to combine technical analysis with other forms of analysis and take a holistic approach to trading and investing.

As a retail trader, it is important to keep a close eye on the decisions made by institutional traders. They often deploy large investment funds, which can create massive liquidity in the markets. Their strategic entry or exit into specific positions can heavily impact market prices, creating new confluences or disrupting existing ones.

The key to identifying these confluences lies in keeping abreast of the actions taken by institutional traders. This can be achieved through research, data analysis, and monitoring market sentiment through news outlets and social media channels. Once a confluence is identified, traders can utilize their technical analysis tools to act quickly and effectively. With accurate identification of such confluences, traders can make informed decisions and potentially reap great rewards by securing a profit before the institutional traders' impact diminishes.

TAKEAWAYS

The advent of advanced technologies has transformed the world of trading. With the assistance of software and algorithms, technical analysis has become more accessible to traders, as it performs complex calculations and simplifies charting activities to help them understand and use this information to their advantage. This has enabled institutional trading strategies to be utilized by retail traders, empowering them to make informed decisions based on sets of simple rules. These automated systems have boosted the efficiency of technical analysis in complex trading scenarios, ultimately allowing retail traders to identify confluences more easily and quickly so they get closer to institutional decision-making. We will discuss these types of software later in the book.

CONCLUSION

Catalysts and confluences play a crucial role in trading and investing. Economic data releases, geopolitical events, corporate earnings, central bank decisions, and technical analysis indicators are interconnected and can collectively impact the financial markets. As traders and investors, it is important to recognize the significance of these factors and how they can converge to create a confluence of events that may significantly affect market movements.

By analysing each variable individually and as part of the bigger picture, we can better predict market movements and make informed decisions. Therefore, a deep understanding of catalysts and confluences is essential for traders and investors looking to succeed and achieve their financial objectives.

CHAPTER 4

Historical Confluences and Market Activity

SOME PEOPLE THINK trading is a little bit like trying to predict the future. I don't entirely disagree, but data analysis and confluences can remove some of this inherent uncertainty. Confluences work to help traders make better forward-looking decisions. Interestingly, another way to inform these forward-looking decisions is by looking backwards. Historical data provides a wealth of information that can help traders identify trends, backtest theories, identify historical volatility, and more.

Confluences play a significant role in the world of trading and investing, and this chapter reflects on historical examples of confluences in market activity. These are the moments when multiple factors come together to create an opportunity or risk in the financial markets. Understanding these past events allows traders and investors to learn to identify future confluences and patterns.

For easy reference, I've ordered these important financial events chronologically. I also tried to select a range of events to illustrate different types of confluence in order to underscore the critical role of multiple economic indicators in the financial markets. These are also events that I have lived through and experienced first-hand.

ASIAN FINANCIAL CRISIS

The Asian financial crisis erupted during the summer of 1997 and spread quickly through several Asian economies, including Thailand, South Korea, Indonesia, and Malaysia.

At this time, the region was experiencing rapid industrialization and had attracted significant capital inflows. However, these investments also created high levels of debt in many countries, and local banks struggled to service foreign debt.

The crisis started with the devaluation of Thailand's currency, the baht, in July 1997. This triggered a chain reaction as other countries began to devalue their currencies to stay competitive. The devaluations led to a sharp decline in the value of assets, such as stocks and real estate, and caused significant hardship for businesses and individuals.

At the same time, the Asian region was hit by other external shocks, including a falling demand for commodities and rising interest rates in the United States. These factors put additional pressure on the already fragile economies, creating a perfect confluence of factors that led to the crisis.

The central banks in the region initially tried to intervene by maintaining exchange rates but failed to stem the tide of currency devaluations. The crisis soon spread to other emerging markets, prompting a worldwide financial meltdown.

LESSONS LEARNED

The Asian financial crisis highlights the importance of confluences in financial markets and how they can have a profound impact. One factor on its own may not have caused the crisis, but the combination of several triggers led to a disastrous outcome. Traders and investors need to be aware of these risks and opportunities and use technical and fundamental analysis to spot confluences before they develop.

The Asian Financial Crisis also demonstrates the critical importance of monitoring multiple factors at once, such as economic data, geopolitics, and market sentiment. Investors and traders should always be vigilant, looking for these confluences and adjusting their strategies accordingly.

In the words of Warren Buffet, "Someone is sitting in the shade today because someone planted a tree a long time ago." By spotting these confluences, traders can plant the seeds today that will bear fruit tomorrow.

2007–2008 GLOBAL FINANCIAL CRISIS

Another example of a confluence in the financial markets that had far-reaching consequences is the 2007–2008 global financial crisis. It was caused by a combination of interconnected market factors that created a perfect storm, leading to the meltdown of the financial markets. This event had far-reaching consequences across the global economy, changing the face of how the financial markets operate today.

The crisis was primarily driven by three interconnected factors: subprime mortgages, complex financial instruments, and a global credit bubble. The United States housing market had experienced a widespread rise in property prices, leading to the rapid growth of subprime mortgages. These mortgages were given to individuals with poor credit ratings, and lenders frequently granted them on terms that were impossible for the borrowers to meet in the long term.

The lending practices that fuelled the growth of subprime mortgages were based on the assumption that property prices would always increase, a belief that proved to be ill-founded. As property prices began to decline in 2006, an increasing number of subprime borrowers began defaulting on their mortgages. This led to the collapse of many financial institutions that had invested heavily in the subprime mortgage market.

Complex financial instruments, such as collateralized debt obligations (CDOs) and credit default swaps (CDSs), were also significant contributors to the crisis. These instruments were created to help investors spread risk and protect themselves against potential losses. However, they also made it challenging to understand the true level of risk associated with specific assets and the overall financial system.

Furthermore, the growth of the global credit bubble created a sense of complacency within the financial markets. Many investors believed that the boom was set to continue unabated, leading to a bumper year of profits for those who invested in risky assets. However, as the subprime mortgage crisis began to unfold, it soon became clear how interconnected the global financial markets were.

As the crisis began to spread throughout the financial markets, many investors began to move their money into

safe assets, such as U.S. Treasury bonds. This led to a pan-
icked sell-off of riskier assets, causing a sharp decline in
asset prices. The sell-off led to the collapse of several large
financial institutions, including Lehman Brothers, Bear
Stearns, and AIG.

In the aftermath of the crisis, regulations were introduced to prevent a repeat of these events. New regulations included The Dodd-Frank Act, which was signed
into law in 2010 and was one of the most impactful of
the new regulations. The Act aimed to reduce the risks
associated with complex financial instruments, such as
CDOs and CDSs.

LESSONS LEARNED

The 2007–2008 global financial crisis is a stark reminder of
how interconnected the financial markets often are and how
devastating the consequences of a confluence of factors can
be. It was a wake-up call for investors and regulators alike,
highlighting the need for a more transparent and regulated
financial system.

The 2007–2008 global financial crisis was a prime example of confluence in the financial markets. Subprime mortgages, complex financial instruments, and a global credit
bubble created an environment of complacency that led to a
global meltdown of the financial markets. In the aftermath
of the crisis, regulations were introduced to prevent a repeat
of the events. Today, the financial markets operate under a
more regulated and transparent system, with a greater focus
on managing risk and maintaining stability.

OPEC OIL PRICE CRASH 2014–2015

The OPEC oil price crash of 2014–2015 was a historic event that significantly affected the energy sector worldwide. A confluence of external factors was responsible for this sudden crash that caught even the most seasoned traders and investors off guard.

Saudi Arabia, the world's largest oil exporter, typically acts as a market stabilizer. But in November 2014, the Saudi government decided to let the oil market balance itself and maintained its production levels despite plummeting demand. This decision turned out to be a highly controversial one, with serious implications for the global economy.

The sudden drop in crude oil prices led to an unforeseen supply glut, which left oil producers with huge surpluses of crude oil supplies. This resulted in negative consequences that were felt worldwide, stretching from energy stocks to consumer prices.

In addition, central banks in oil-exporting countries adopted policies, such as reduced interest rates and monetary easing measures, to prevent the economic downturn from worsening. However, these measures failed to have the desired impact, leading to a significant and prolonged recession in several oil-dependent economies.

LESSONS LEARNED

The OPEC oil price crash of 2014–2015 provides an essential lesson on the importance of understanding confluences when trading or investing in the financial markets. In the case of the OPEC oil price crash, the confluences were made up of the production decisions of the Saudi Arabian government, the changing dynamics of global energy production, and the regulatory policies of central banks in oil-producing countries. These factors together created significant changes in market prices that resulted in the sudden price collapse. The confluence of these external factors impacted the energy sector worldwide. It serves as a valuable lesson on the importance of understanding confluences and staying informed about emerging market trends and developments. Being alert to potential pitfalls and opportunities can help investors make smarter and more profitable investment decisions.

BREXIT

Undoubtedly, Brexit is one of the most significant examples of a confluence of events that have impacted the financial markets in recent years. The referendum result in June 2016, where 52 percent of Britons voted to leave the European Union (EU), created a ripple effect that was felt across the globe.

The uncertainty surrounding Britain's future outside the EU created a sense of unease among investors, leading to a drop in the value of the British pound. The pound fell to its lowest level against the US dollar in more than thirty years, causing havoc in the financial markets. Many investors started to withdraw their investments from the United Kingdom (UK), and major financial institutions, such as banks and insurance companies, started moving their operations to other countries.

The political turmoil that ensued further compounded the problem. There was a leadership crisis in the UK that led to the resignation of Prime Minister David Cameron and the subsequent appointment of Theresa May. This uncertainty added to the challenges that investors had to face, and the financial markets became extremely volatile.

To mitigate the impact of Brexit on the financial markets, the Bank of England (BOE) intervened by cutting interest rates to their lowest levels in history. This move was intended to stimulate economic growth and provide liquidity to the markets. The BOE also signalled further monetary easing, including quantitative easing and the purchase of government bonds, to help stabilize the market.

The BOE's response proved to be effective, as it helped to prevent a deeper recession. The UK's economic growth, though sluggish, did not fall below the predicted levels, and the financial markets stabilized. However, the impact of Brexit is still being felt, and the long-term consequences of the decision are yet to be determined.

LESSONS LEARNED

Brexit is a prime example of how a confluence of events can have a profound impact on the financial markets. The UK's decision to leave the EU created a sense of uncertainty among investors, leading to a drop in the value of the pound and a subsequent drop in the financial markets. The BOE's response by cutting the interest rates to their lowest levels in history and signalling further monetary easing was crucial in stabilizing the market and preventing a deeper recession.

Nevertheless, the long-term consequences of Brexit on the financial markets are still being determined, and investors need to remain vigilant as the situation evolves.

PRESIDENT TRUMP AND CHINA 2018

Towards the end of 2018, the global market witnessed yet another confluence that had a major impact on trading and investing in the financial markets. It started when President Trump launched a trade war with China, which created an atmosphere of instability and unpredictability in the global economy. As a result, global demand for commodities plummeted, which had a significant impact on the stock market.

At the same time, the U.S. Federal Reserve raised interest rates, which further exacerbated the situation. Historically, interest rate hikes tend to have a negative impact on the stock market as they increase the cost of borrowing. This is because when interest rates rise, companies may find it more difficult to secure funding for their growth plans and expansion strategies, which can hinder their profitability and long-term prospects.

Given the trade war with China and the interest rate hike, there was a perfect storm brewing that had the potential to wreak havoc on the US stock market. Not surprisingly, the stock market saw sharp declines, with the S&P 500 and Dow Jones indexes losing around 15 percent of their value in the last quarter of 2018.

One of the crucial factors that made this confluence particularly challenging was its far-reaching impact. Since the trade war between the US and China is a global issue, its impact was not limited to just one region or country. Instead, it had knock-on effects on all major economies and their respective stock markets.

Another factor that played a role in this confluence was the timing of the interest rate hike. The Federal Reserve's decision to raise interest rates in the midst of a global economic slowdown was seen by many as a misstep. Critics argue that the Fed should have been more cautious and waited until the global economy had stabilized before raising interest rates.

LESSONS LEARNED

Despite these challenges, however, many investors managed to weather the storm. One of the strategies that proved successful was diversification across different asset classes, such as bonds and commodities, as a way of spreading the risk and reducing exposure to any single market. Additionally, some investors chose to take a longer-term view and exercise patience, waiting for the market to stabilize before making any significant moves.

The confluence at the end of 2018 serves as a reminder of the importance of staying informed and vigilant when it comes to investing and trading in the financial markets. It underscores the need to consider all relevant factors, both macro and micro, and to adopt a diversified approach that takes into account different market conditions and asset classes. By staying informed and adopting a disciplined and patient approach, investors and traders can navigate even the most challenging market conditions.

CONCLUSION

As traders and investors, it's crucial to be mindful of how current and historical confluences can impact the financial markets. In each economic event discussed, multiple factors came together to create an opportunity or risk in the financial markets. Understanding the confluences that led to these past events can help traders and investors identify future confluences and patterns.

Additionally, it's essential to watch for emerging trends and developments in the markets that can help an investor identify potential risks and opportunities. For instance, the COVID-19 pandemic is another event that had a big impact on the financial markets. The global recession that resulted from the pandemic created similar confluences of factors that caused the aviation, oil, and hospitality sectors to crash significantly.

Staying alert to confluences can help you to anticipate and avoid potential financial losses. You can achieve this by rigorously monitoring the performance of indicators that can influence market performance (such as macroeconomic data and key commodities) and by keeping a watchful eye on the major players in the market.

As an investor, always be prepared for the unexpected and be flexible enough to adapt to changing market conditions. This adaptability, combined with the understanding of how confluences can impact the financial markets, can be a powerful tool for maximizing portfolio returns and minimizing financial risks.

SECTION 3

CONFLUENCE AND TRADING STRATEGIES

CHAPTER 5

Technical Starting Strategies

WHEN IT COMES to trading and investing in the financial markets, the options can seem endless. But, for the purposes of this book, we will delve into just two types of trading and strategies — day trading futures and swing trading or investing in stocks.

First, we'll explore day trading futures. This strategy involves buying and selling futures contracts within the same trading day. The goal is to profit from small price movements. It is a high-risk, high-reward approach that requires quick decision-making, precise timing, and a thorough understanding of market trends. Day trading futures can be particularly appealing to those who seek to make quick profits and are comfortable with a more aggressive trading style. More on this in chapter 6.

The second type of trading we will examine is swing trading or investing in stocks. This strategy involves holding positions for a longer period of time, typically days or weeks, in order to profit from larger price movements. Swing traders and investors tend to take a more conservative approach, as they seek to capture a larger portion of a trend rather than make quick profits. This approach requires a patient mindset as well as an ability to analyse and interpret market data to make well-informed decisions. We will discuss this in more depth in chapter 7.

SETTING THE OPERATIONAL LANDSCAPE

Before diving into the details of trading strategies, it's important to talk about the operational landscape — what it means and how you define it.

I developed an understanding of operational landscape and its relevance whilst working as an engineering manager with the British Army. During this time, I coordinated large-scale projects and managed complicated logistical plans. My first instinct when it came to making decisions on equipment movement or team deployment was to assess the overall operational landscape. I evaluated the big picture and took a holistic view of the operation before deciding on the best course of action.

Operations in military settings can be highly unpredictable and subject to constant change, requiring a fluid approach to decision-making and a comprehensive understanding of how different elements converge to impact the situation. When considering the movement of equipment or deployment of repair teams, I had to take into account a confluence of factors, such as the time required for repairs, the fluid nature of the operation, and the potential for disruptions and impediments.

To make sound decisions, it remains essential to gather data from various sources and evaluate the situation from multiple perspectives. One must consider all of the potential factors that could play a role in the successful execution of the operation. This requires a deep understanding of the interplay between different elements, such as how various repairs might impact the operational timeline or the potential risks and complications that could arise from equipment movement, deployment, or maintenance.

Sounds a lot like trading, yes?

FRAMING A TRADING CHART

To identify your operational landscape, it is important to understand the concept of framing a trading chart, specifically by looking for confluences with linear and non-linear support and resistance zones. Support and resistance in trading refer to key zones on a chart where the price tends to experience a barrier. At these points, price stops either increasing further or declining lower, respectively, due to the presence of significant buying or selling pressure from market participants.

Framing a trading chart involves visualizing key levels of price action over a specified period of time. With this technique, traders can identify support and resistance levels that are crucial for identifying potential buying or selling points. Framing a chart is done by creating straight lines that connect areas of support and resistance on a chart over time, creating an overall picture of price action.

One of the key things to understand about support and resistance is that they aren't set in stone. Instead, they tend to shift and evolve over time as market conditions change. As such, it's good to keep in mind that a support or resistance level that works well in one market environment may not work as well in a different environment.

LINEAR SUPPORT AND RESISTANCE ZONES

Linear support and resistance zones are areas on a chart where prices have consistently bounced off, providing levels of support or resistance. These levels can be created by drawing a horizontal line that connects the lowest or highest points of the price action. Linear support and resistance zones are often used for trading strategies, such as breakouts and pullbacks, when price moves beyond these levels. It's important to remember that linear support and resistance zones are not fixed and may change over time as new price levels are established.

Additionally, support and resistance can be taken from multiple timeframes. For example, a trader might look at a daily chart to identify support and resistance levels, but they might also look at a weekly or monthly chart to see if there are any support or resistance levels that are visible across multiple timeframes. When confluences of support or resistance zones occur across multiple timeframes, it suggests a strong zone of support or resistance.

Looking at support and resistance taken from multiple timeframes provides powerful insights because the levels represent areas of the market where a large number of traders are likely to be focused. For example, if there is a support level at $100 that is visible on both a daily and a weekly chart, this suggests that a large number of traders are likely to be watching this level. If the price of the asset falls to this level, these traders may enter the market to buy, which could push the price back up.

As we come to the first chart in the book, a note about visual quality. Although I have selected premium colour paper and printing for this book, analogue images are not as clear as digital ones. To access clear digital images, I've created a free book club for readers as a resource. Go to PaulBratby.com/Book-Club to view all the charts in this book on your computer, laptop, or tablet.

Let's take a day trading example. Take a look at Chart 5.1, which illustrates an instrument on a 5-minute timeframe. The yellow support and resistance zones are the native 5-minute timeframe. The turquoise is a 15-minute timeframe, and the green is a 30-minute timeframe. The pink shows the 60-minute timeframe support and resistance zones.

In the centre of the chart, we can observe the phenomenon of a confluence of all timeframes forming strong support and resistance. When a parabolic move breaks down below such a support zone, it indicates that significant economic data has been released to the market, causing the price to drop. This catalyst can be powerful enough to push through the support zone. However, when the same confluence zone is tested from below, we observe that it now acts as strong resistance, around which price tends to fluctuate.

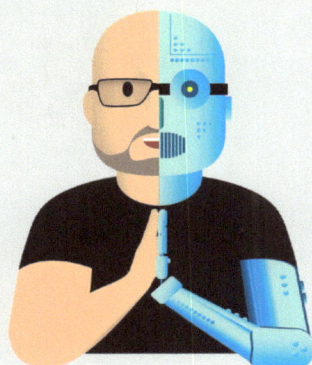

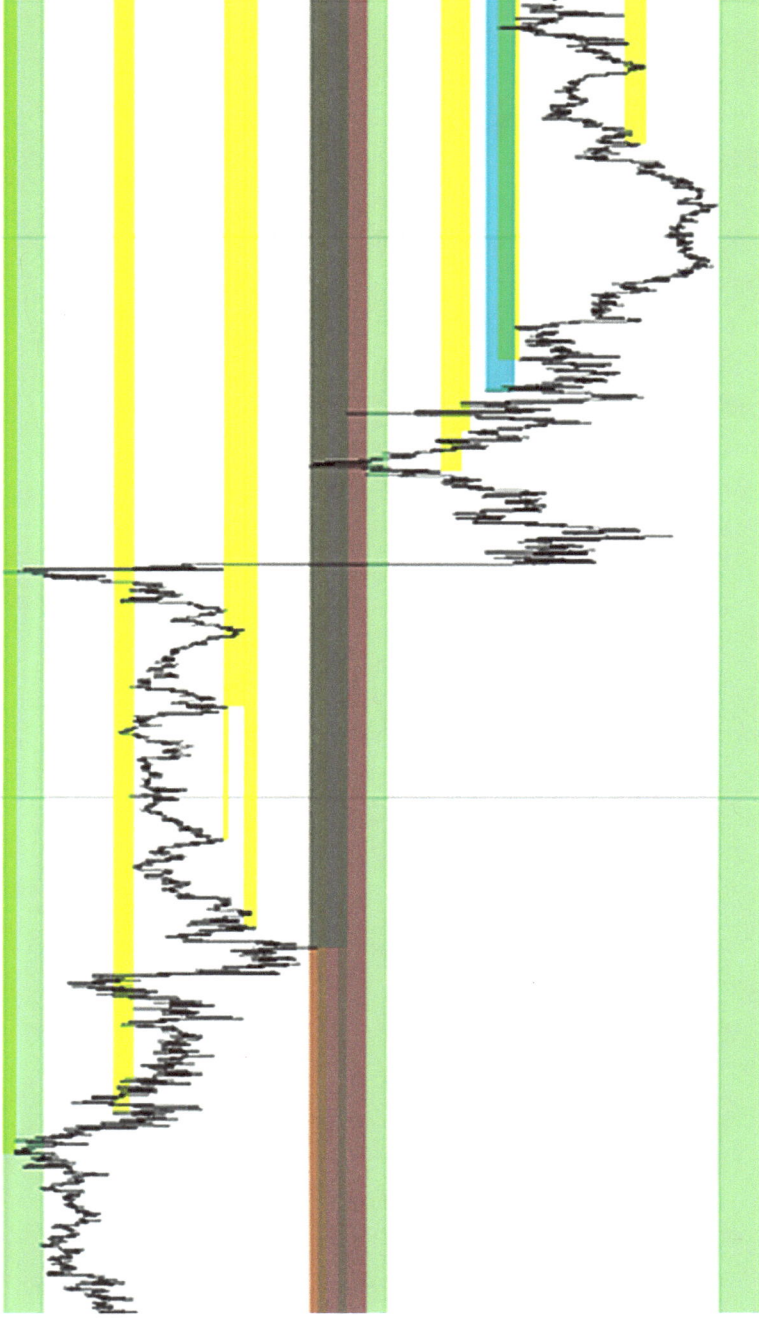

Chart 5.1 – Multi Timeframe Linear Support and Resistance Zones.

One of the advantages of having multiple timeframe support and resistance zones on a single chart is that they allow traders to visualize these confluences quickly and conveniently. This, in turn, helps them understand the additional confluence of economic data that pushes the price through the support zone. Armed with this knowledge, traders can capitalize on trading opportunities in the market to the downside when the confluence zone is tested from below and rejected.

By applying a thorough understanding of the multiple timeframes present on a trading chart, traders adopt a holistic approach to market movement. They can analyse the current market trends, identify potential support and resistance areas, and develop a trading plan that takes into consideration the larger picture of the market. The use of multiple timeframes can also help traders filter out market noise, allowing them to spot market trends with greater clarity and confidence.

NON-LINEAR SUPPORT AND RESISTANCE ZONES

Non-linear support and resistance zones, on the other hand, are not created by straight horizontal lines and instead rely on trendlines and channels to determine levels of support and resistance. Non-linear support and resistance zones are often used to identify trending markets where prices are moving in a clear direction, allowing traders to participate in the trend by buying at support levels and selling at resistance levels. Non-linear support and resistance ones can be more effective than linear ones for traders looking to capitalize on long-term trends. But when there is confluence between both, traders must take notice.

TREND CHANNELS

A trend channel is a graphic representation of a trend drawn on a larger timeframe than the one in which trading is taking place. Traders use this tool to identify confluences or touches at the bottom of the trend line pivots in order to form the lower bound of the trend channel. The same process is repeated for the upper bound of the channel.

When constructing the trend channel, traders are typically looking for the biggest confluence to occur around the centre line of the channel. This line can be viewed as the "line of best fit" for the trend direction and angle. This is because the centre line represents the average price level for the security in question and, therefore, acts as a key psychological barrier that traders may look to exploit.

A key benefit of the trend channel is that it can help traders identify potential support and resistance levels for a given security. For example, if the price of a security bounces off the lower end of the channel several times, this can be seen as a strong support level. Conversely, if the price of the security consistently fails to breach the upper end of the channel, this could be viewed as a strong resistance level.

Another advantage of the trend channel is that it can help traders identify potential buy or sell signals based on the behaviour of the security within the channel. For example, if the price of a security breaks through the upper bound of the channel, this could be seen as a signal to buy. Conversely, if the price falls below the lower bound of the channel, this could be viewed as a signal to sell.

In Chart 5.2, the same instrument discussed earlier on the chart has been taken to the 60-minute timeframe where two distinct trend channels have been drawn. These channels, consisting of the upper and lower bounds, can be utilized to identify the range in which the instrument is trading. Notably, the upper and lower bounds have strong confluences with multiple touches and tests indicating that these levels are critical points of resistance and support, respectively.

Perhaps even more critical are the confluences on the centre lines, represented by the red-dashed lines. These lines are calculated using the "line of best fit" approach in engineering terminology. They depict the path of the trend and can be invaluable in determining the underlying direction of an instrument's price. In this specific example, the confluences on the centre lines are particularly noteworthy, indicating the strength of the trend.

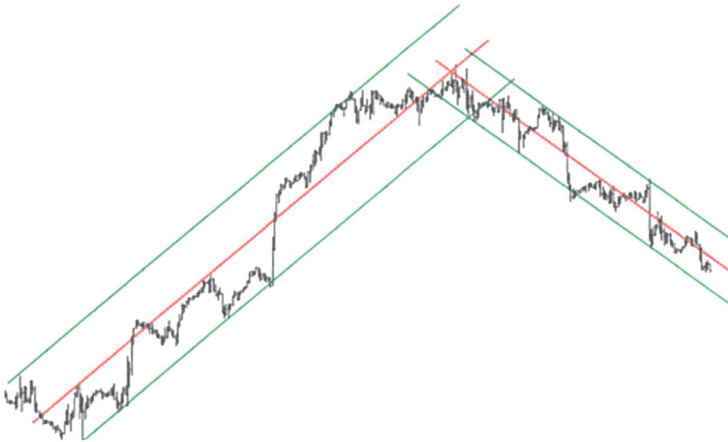

Chart 5.2 – Trend Channels.

It is worth noting that the trend channel should never be considered in isolation. Instead, it should be used in conjunction with other technical analysis tools and fundamental analysis data to provide a more complete picture of the market trends and potential trading opportunities.

Looking at the original 5-minute timeframe, it is evident that the intersection of the non-linear upper bound of the trend channel with the 5-, 15- and 30-minute resistance zones (yellow, turquoise, and green, respectively) just before an economic data reaction was no mere coincidence. In fact, it was a perfect alignment of factors that led to a massive parabolic move down, affecting the market deeply.

It is worth noting that the confluence of economic data reaction and both linear and non-linear support and resistance was a significant contributor to this perfect storm. The impact was so profound that the big move broke through really strong linear support and then found support at the lower bound of the trend channel before coming back up to test the same massive multi-timeframe confluence zone as resistance.

To emphasize this point further, it is worth noting that a bearish move begins to take place in the lower half of the trend channel. This movement shows traders that there is no real appetite in the markets to push the price of this asset higher. Therefore, it is essential to note that long trades are incredibly high-risk at this moment in time.

OTHER USES FOR SUPPORT AND RESISTANCE

It's also worth noting that support and resistance levels can be used in a variety of different trading strategies. For example, traders might use support and resistance levels as entry and exit points for their trades. They might look to buy an asset when it hits a support level and sell it when it hits a resistance level. Alternatively, they might use support and

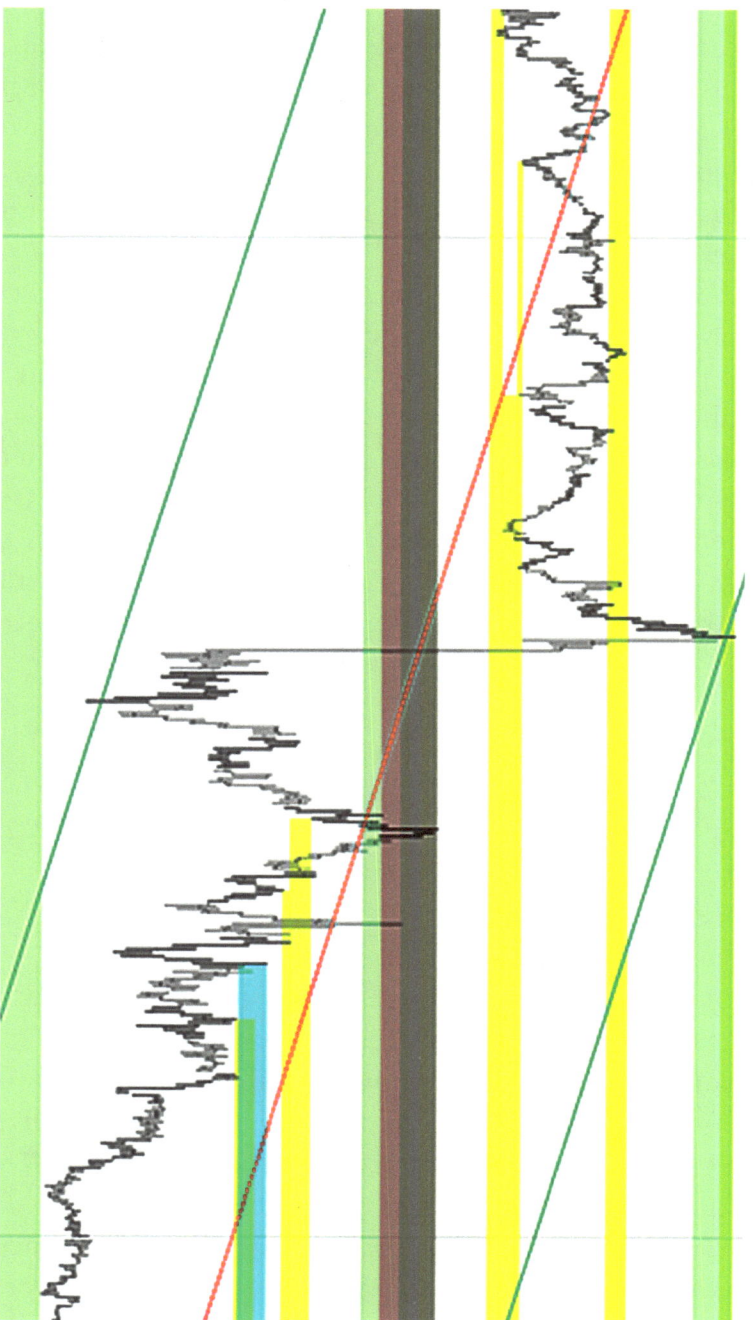

Chart 5.3 – Confluences of Linear and Non-Linear Support and Resistance.

resistance levels to set stop-loss orders, which can help limit their losses if the market moves against them. In Chart 5.3, it is obvious that many traders put buy orders in or around the lower bound of the trend channel as the reaction back up to test the linear confluence zone was significant. Then, sell orders were obviously placed in that same confluence zone.

Another possible use for support and resistance levels is to predict potential price movements, as can be seen in Chart 5.4. For example, if a trader notices that an asset has been bouncing around between two key support and resistance levels for an extended period of time, they might predict that the price will continue to move within this range. On the other hand, if the price breaks through a key support or resistance level, this might indicate a major shift in market sentiment and a potential opportunity to enter a new trade.

MOVING AVERAGES

Another non-linear support and resistance visualisation is the moving average (MA) and exponential moving average (EMA), which are both designed to help traders identify levels of support and resistance.

A moving average is a simple arithmetic mean of a selected number of prices over a specified time period. The formula for calculating a moving average involves summing up the prices for a particular time period and then dividing the sum by the number of prices in the time period. The resulting value is then plotted on the trading chart.

On the other hand, the exponential moving average (EMA) is a more complex moving average indicator that

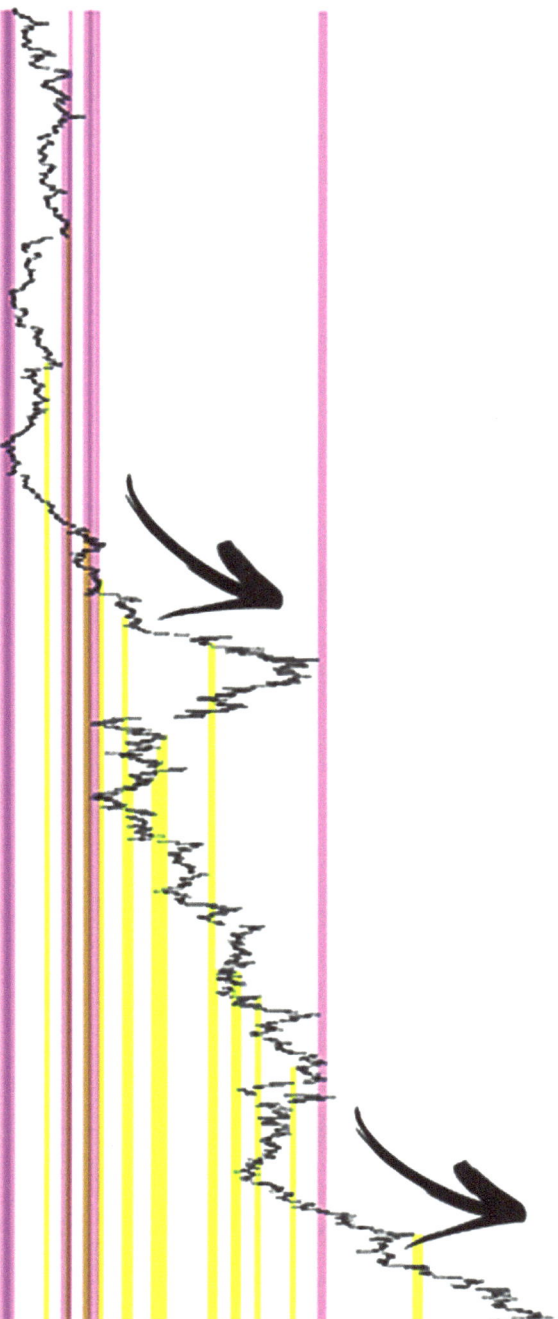

Chart 5.4 – Respecting or Breaking Through Support or Resistance.

places greater weight on more recent prices than on older prices. This is done by using a smoothing factor that gives more importance to the most recent data points.

The difference between these two types of moving averages lies mainly in the way they are calculated, the time period used, and the weighting factors assigned to each data point. While a simple moving average provides traders with a general idea of the trend, an exponential moving average is believed to be more sensitive to price changes, and therefore, it is considered to be more effective in identifying short-term trend changes.

One of the main advantages of using moving averages and EMA on a trading chart is that they help traders identify areas of non-linear support and resistance. These levels of support and resistance are critical as they represent psychological barriers that traders often react to. When the price approaches a level of support, there is a higher likelihood that buyers will enter the market, while at resistance levels, sellers will be more inclined to enter.

Non-linear areas of support and resistance tend to be harder to identify, and this is where EMAs can be useful. By smoothing out the price data, these technical indicators help traders recognise trend changes and areas of potential reversals more easily. These points of inflection can be used for entry and exit signals and provide traders with dynamic information on when to take profits. By continually analysing the price action and adjusting their orders accordingly, traders can maximize their profits while minimizing their risk.

Chart 5.5 graphs the daily timeframe of the S&P500 Index. We can see two EMA clouds — a grey one representing the 55

EMA and a magenta one representing the 89 EMA.

The grey cloud's upper bound is derived from the 55 EMA highs and the lower bound from the lows, while the magenta cloud follows the same theory. By observing their confluences with price action, we can draw conclusions about the strength of a trend.

When the 55 EMA cloud is situated above the 89 EMA cloud, and there is a notable gap between them, we can confidently say that the instrument is in a strong bullish trend. On the other hand, when the 55 EMA cloud falls below and clears the 89 EMA cloud, it signifies a bearish trend.

Another indicator tool I've created is the EMA Cloud Indicator, which is also included with the purchase of this book. This indicator is a useful way to view non-linear support and resistance data and can be applied to multiple timeframes.

Utilizing the EMA cloud technique, as opposed to individual EMA lines, provides traders and investors with a clearer visual representation of non-linear support

Scan me!

Introducing the
FREE xBrat EMA Cloud Indicator

Check out all the trading platforms the **xBrat EMA Cloud Indicator** is available for, by scanning the QR Code above.

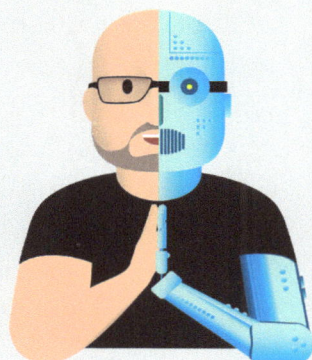

and resistance zones. By examining Chart 5.5, it is evident that a robust bullish trend exists, visually indicating a recovery after the devastating COVID-19 pandemic pullback, which can be seen towards the lower left of the chart. For swing trading and investing purposes, I have used the combination of 55 and 89 EMAs since 2013. The 55 EMA cloud serves as a standard non-linear support during longer-term trends, while the 89 EMA cloud acts as a "last chance saloon" non-linear support.

This pragmatic approach helps traders remain calm during shallow pullbacks, as evidenced by the numerous tests of the grey 55 EMA cloud on the chart. During more substantial pullbacks, the robustness of the 89 EMA cloud provides a sturdy point of inflection and support. The utilization of these EMA clouds offers traders and investors vital information and enables them to make informed decisions and confident investments.

CONFLUENCES AROUND THE 2'S

Now, looking at Chart 5.6, let's add the rest of our framing work to this S&P500 Daily chart and identify confluences that could be useful in the future. First, number 1 identifies the COVID-19 pandemic pullback of not just the S&P500 but also the financial markets as a whole, specifically from the middle of February 2020 until the end of March 2020. We are going to discuss this pullback with more clarity in the swing trading chapter later in this book.

The initial recovery impulse moves up from the pandemic pullback and pushes the price of the S&P500 through the

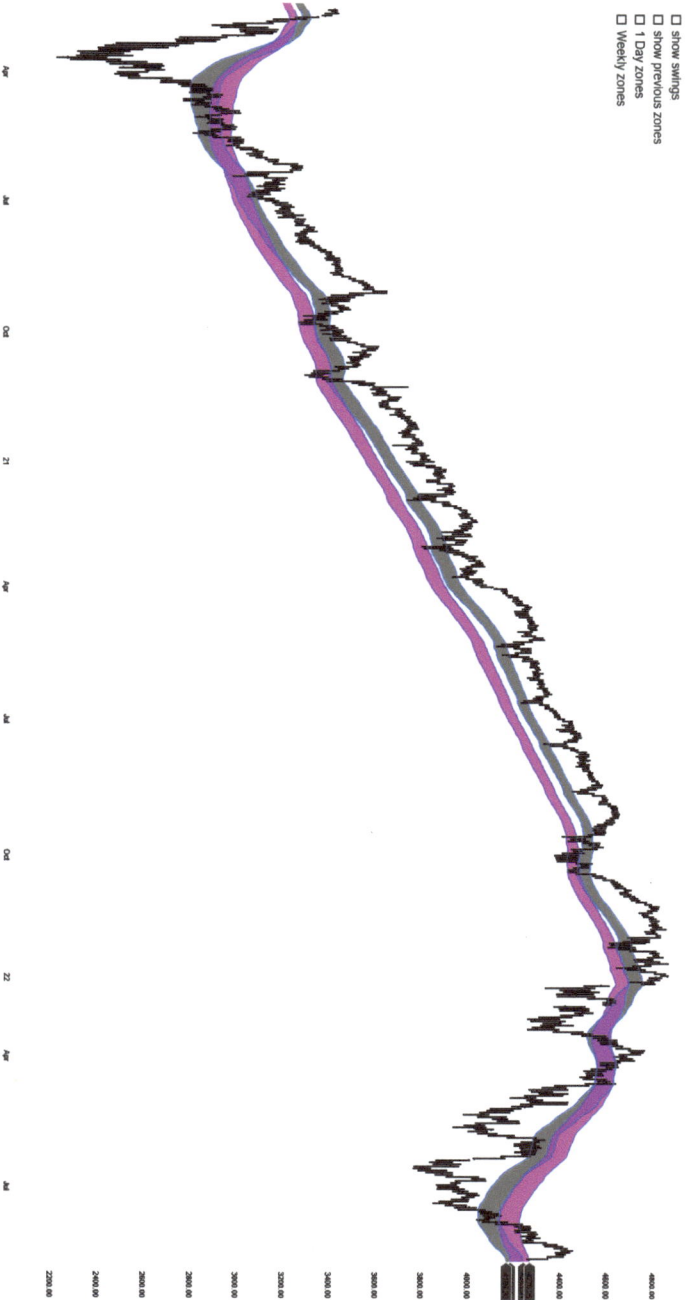

Chart 5.5 – Exponential Moving Average Support and Resistance

55 and 89 EMA clouds, finding strong resistance at the first point from the left — labelled number 2. At this point, the price comes back down to test the confluence of both 55 and 89 EMA clouds. It finds support and pushes to break the high pivot of that first number 2 resistance. Then, for the next two weeks, a period of clustering occurs around this zone, which gives us our second number 2. The next bullish impulse move takes place until it finds resistance at around $3,600. Now, we start to see the formation of the longer-term trend channel highlighted in the chart.

The pullback down from here is very significant and tests the new linear support and resistance zone formed by the first pair of number 2s and the 89 EMA cloud. At this point, the confluence of both linear and non-linear support is enough for investors to buy and forms the third number 2 on the chart. The price moves higher until it finds resistance at the centre line (red-dashed line) of the newly formed trend channel. A fourth test of this begins, and strong support for our fourth number 2 holds. Traders now gain more confidence that market sentiment does not want to push this price down, enabling a good, strong bullish run with the price predominantly remaining in the lower bound of the bullish trend channel until the next test of the 89 EMA cloud in March 2021.

The first test of the 89 EMA cloud that tries to break down out of the bullish trend channel fails, and the price moves back into the channel to continue its bullish trajectory. This zone should be noted by traders and extended into the future as a strong support zone. As you can see on the right of Chart 5.6 and as shown by the other number 3s, this zone of support was confirmed after the

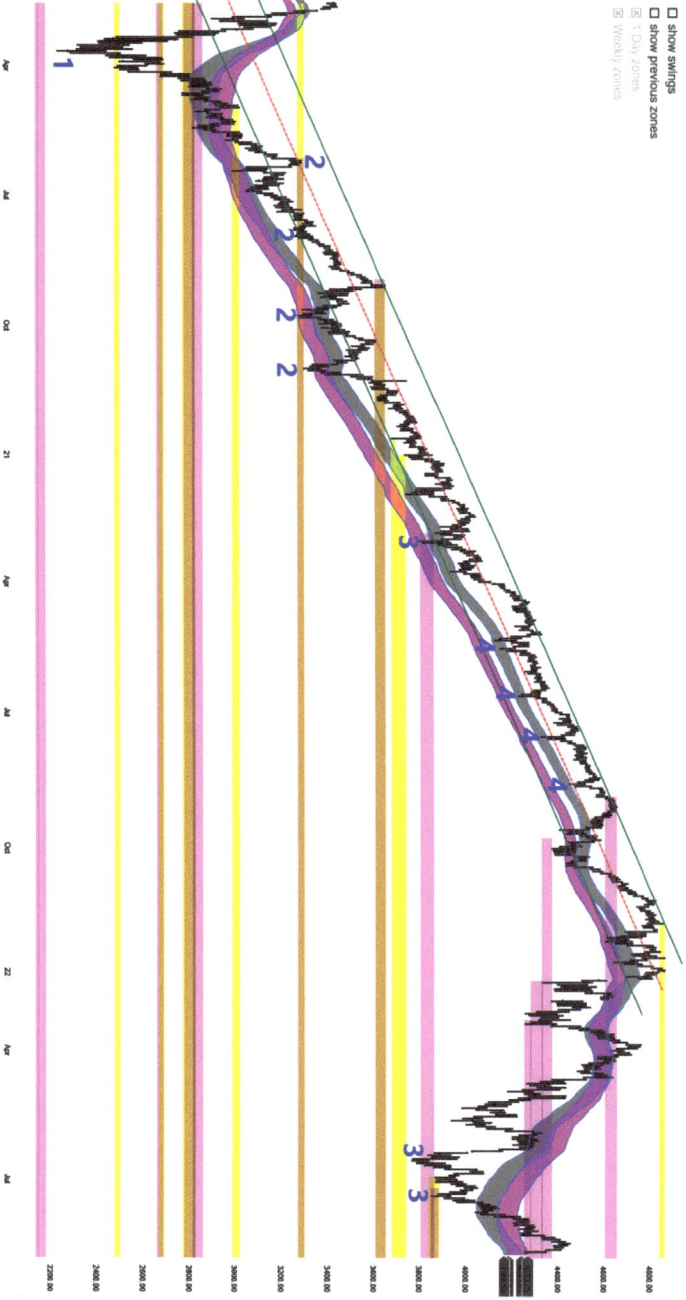

Chart 5.6 – EMA Clouds on S&P500 Daily Chart Through COVID-19 Recovery.

show swings
show previous zones
1 Day zones
Weekly zones

bearish pullback initiated by the Russian invasion of Ukraine in February 2022. A geopolitical event reaction confirms strong support. Many confluences are at play here. This zone of price for the S&P500 is very strong and should be treated as such by traders in the future.

Let's just touch on the number 4s. These provide clarification of the main non-linear EMA cloud support in a strong bullish trend in this case.

CONCLUSION

As you can see, one of the most important aspects of framing a chart is the notion of confluences. Confluences refer to the alignment of multiple factors, including key support and resistance levels, patterns, trendlines, and other technical indicators. Tracking these elements can indicate to traders any potential entry, exit, or reversal points. The more confluences that are present, the greater the likelihood of a trade's success and the lower the risk of failure.

CHAPTER 6

Day Trading and Confluences

DAY TRADING FUTURES contracts is one of the most popular trading and investing approaches in the world of financial markets. This trading strategy involves buying and selling futures contracts to take advantage of any small price fluctuations in the futures markets within a single trading day. As such, it requires traders to closely monitor various technical indicators and economic data points to help identify profitable trades. It is an aggressive trading style that offers a high-risk, high-reward approach. In this chapter, we will discuss the main confluences involved with day trading futures contracts, particularly in relation to gold futures, oil futures, US index futures, and a surprise appearance by soybean futures.

When day trading futures contracts, technical indicators can help forecast the future direction of an asset's price. They are mathematical calculations based on an instrument or asset's price and/or volume. When day trading futures contracts, the most commonly used technical indicators include moving averages, relative strength index (RSI), stochastic oscillator, and the MACD. Technical indicators can be used to identify trend direction, momentum, and entry and exit points.

On the other hand, economic data points are information releases that are relevant to the financial markets. These data points can provide traders with information on the state of the economy, which can help them make better trading decisions. Some examples of economic data points that are commonly monitored by day traders include gross domestic product (GDP), the consumer price index (CPI), interest rates, and unemployment rates.

THE ONLY ADVICE I EVER GIVE DAY TRADERS!

Technical indicators and economic data points provide raw data, but traders need to follow a bigger strategy. When day trading futures, stocks, forex, or even crypto, it is crucial to understand the behaviour of one instrument — only one. Develop an intimate understanding of how this instrument reacts to economic data. Know and understand its strong correlations as well as its external and internal confluences. Determine the best times of the day to trade it and, conversely, when it is best NOT to trade it.

Over the last nine years, many traders have gotten in touch with me to say they can't make their trading strategies work. I found a common theme in their struggles. They were all trying to trade, on average, five different instruments! It has to be only one instrument.

To make my point, I ask them only one question, "How many spouses do you have?"

They always answer, "One."

I then ask, "Do you think you could cope with five?"

They all quickly reply, "No chance."

So, my obvious reply is, "Then why are you trying to day trade five different instruments?"

In life, it is often better to opt for a monogamous relationship and focus on nurturing a deep understanding of our partner's needs and behaviours. This approach can help foster a sense of intimacy and connection that is often absent in multi-partner relationships.

When it comes to day trading, this same principle applies. It is important to approach day trading with a strategic mindset and focus on one instrument. Attempting to juggle multiple instruments simultaneously can lead to confusion, errors, and missed opportunities. Instead, identifying a single sound instrument and dedicating one's resources and attention to it can be the key to success.

TRADING STRATEGY

Throughout this chapter, I will use various financial instruments as examples to demonstrate the diverse confluences and strategies that can be utilized in the trading world. While there are many options available, I personally only trade copper futures due to the time zone in which I reside and my comprehensive understanding of the behaviours and confluences within this particular market.

By trading in copper futures, I have been able to gain a deep understanding of the unique dynamics at play within this specific market. My familiarity and expertise in this area allow me to make informed decisions that are based on a multitude of factors, including economic indicators, market trends, and historical analysis.

It is important to note that every trader's preference and strategy will differ based on their individual circumstances and desired outcomes. However, by exploring various instruments and markets, traders can gain valuable knowledge and insights that are transferable across various trading platforms.

I will provide detailed examples and analysis of various trading scenarios, highlighting the confluences and strategies that are at play in each. It is my hope that these insights will provide valuable guidance to traders, regardless of their preferred markets or instruments of choice.

Now, let's discuss the confluences between technical indicators and economic data points in day trading futures contracts. These confluences help traders better understand the market's current state, which, in turn, enables them to identify potential trading opportunities.

GOLD FUTURES – $GC

Gold futures are one of the most popular commodities to invest in, with their popularity among investors stemming from their historical value as a safe haven investment. As such, trading gold futures requires a thorough understanding of various technical indicators, market behaviour, economic data points, and range during the European and US gold pit opening times.

TECHNICAL INDICATORS

One of the most commonly used technical indicators in gold futures trading is the **moving average**. This indicator helps traders identify trends, support and resistance levels, and potential entry and exit points. The moving average also helps traders identify optimal trading timeframes, allowing traders to predict the most profitable investments.

Economic data points also play a critical role in gold futures trading. The US dollar has a significant impact on gold prices. A rise in the dollar results in a decrease in gold prices, while a weaker dollar usually leads to an increase in gold prices. As such, traders need to keep a close eye on US economic data releases, such as the CPI, which influence gold price movements.

Apart from technical indicators and economic data points, traders also consider **market behaviour and volume** to gain a better understanding of asset behaviour. For example, it is common for gold futures to experience increased trading volumes at the European and US gold pit opening times. During these opening times, traders also look for breakouts of the initial trading range produced, which can provide useful insights into potential future trends. The xBrat Range Breakout trading software is designed specifically to help traders identify and then trade on these confluences of behaviour.

OPENING RANGE TRADE

The xBrat Range Breakout software focuses on understanding market sentiment to gain an edge in investing and

trading in financial markets. The cutting-edge tool has been specifically developed to provide insight into the bias of market sentiment during the critical first ten minutes after the gold pit opens.

By utilising moving averages and their positions relative to one another, the xBrat Range Breakout calculates fluctuations in market sentiment, providing a clear indication of whether it is bullish, bearish, or even neutral. Based on these fluctuations, an opening range is defined and colour coded. For instance, if a green colour is assigned to the opening range, it indicates a bullish market sentiment.

This unique approach is effective, as it determines both the high and low of the range, allowing traders to take advantage of market sentiment by trading a breakout of the range. By participating in range breakouts in the direction of the market bias, traders can make informed trading decisions that optimise their chances of success. As such, the xBrat Range Breakout tool is particularly useful for day traders, offering them the ability to make informed decisions based on two simple confluences.

As an example, if the opening range is coloured in green, then trading decisions should only entail looking for a long breakout of the range's high.

Chart 6.1 provides a comprehensive illustration of the tool's application, including an example of a 10-minute opening range from 08:20 a.m. to 08:30 a.m. EST, defined and coloured green. In such cases, traders should look to take a long position when the price breaks the high of the opening range. As a reminder, to view a digital version of the charts in this chapter, go to PaulBratby.com/Book-Club.

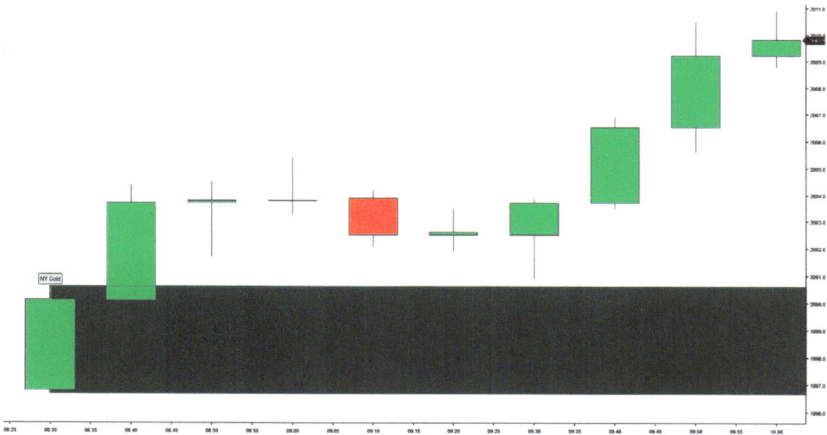

Chart 6.1 – Gold Futures Opening Range Trade.

BIAS ON HIGHER TIMEFRAMES

When it comes to day trading gold futures, it is critical to have a solid strategy in place. One exceptional approach is to investigate the BIAS on higher timeframes

Scan me!

Introducing the
xBrat
BIAS Depth
Heatmap

Check out all the trading platforms the **xBrat BIAS Depth Heatmap** is available for, by scanning the QR Code above.

to obtain a comprehensive overview. This is where the xBrat BIAS Depth heatmap comes into play. Utilizing the same moving average comparisons of the range breakout, this tool examines six timeframes higher than the one currently in focus. By analysing the confluences of these six higher timeframes, traders can gain a more powerful and holistic confirmation of their bullish long setup for gold.

If all six higher timeframes indicate a bullish sentiment through the display of green congruent expansions, the trader can be confident in their position. This confluence serves as a potent confirmation for those looking to trade gold futures. Conversely, if the six higher timeframes don't align, this is a clear sign for the trader to avoid this trade. In this scenario, without confirmation from all six higher timeframes, there is simply too much risk involved.

Overall, implementing the xBrat BIAS Depth heatmap can help traders take their gold futures strategy to the next level. With this tool, traders can gain valuable insight into the critical BIASes on higher timeframes, which can offer a broader perspective and increase the overall accuracy of trades.

Chart 6.2 adds the xBrat BIAS Depth heatmap to the previous chart that illustrates a gold futures opening range trade. The addition of the xBrat BIAS Depth heatmap shows confluence of all six timeframes in the same direction (green bullish colour) as the xBrat Range Breakout. Chart 6.3 is an exploded view of all six timeframes separated.

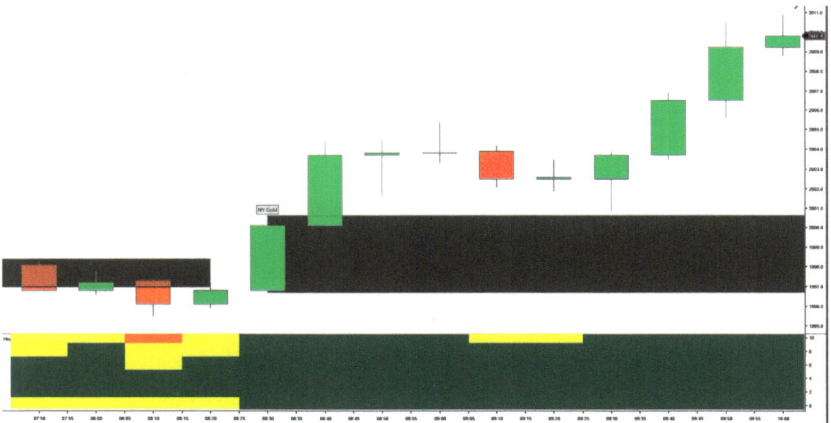

Chart 6.2 – Gold Futures Opening Range chart with xBrat BIAS Depth heatmap added.

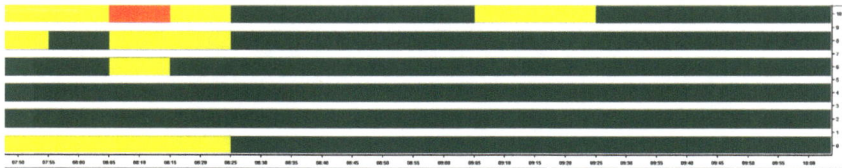

Chart 6.3 – BIAS Depth Heatmap in Detail.

TAKEAWAYS

Combining opening range and BIAS on higher timeframe strategies can help traders optimize their trading decisions and increase their profitability. In addition to market behaviour and volume, traders should also keep an eye on other economic data points, including inflation rates, interest rates, and geopolitical events, which can impact gold prices. Such information provides insight into the future direction of gold futures markets, making it an important aspect of any trader's strategy.

ECONOMIC DATA RELEASES

For economic data releases, certain times and days of the week can prove to be crucial. For instance, large economic data is often released just ten minutes after the US gold pit opens. The reaction to this economic data can tremendously impact the price of gold, thereby presenting both risks and opportunities.

Chart 6.4 starts (the very left of the chart) the day before an economic data release and commences with the opening of the New York gold pit, followed by the downward movement of the price action. However, as we see, the price action finds support at the European gold pit opening range from earlier that day. This occurrence is not by chance but rather a common phenomenon that traders use to their advantage.

As the price becomes range-bound between the two opening ranges, it is typical behaviour and a signal for traders to take action by utilizing the confluence of ranges to

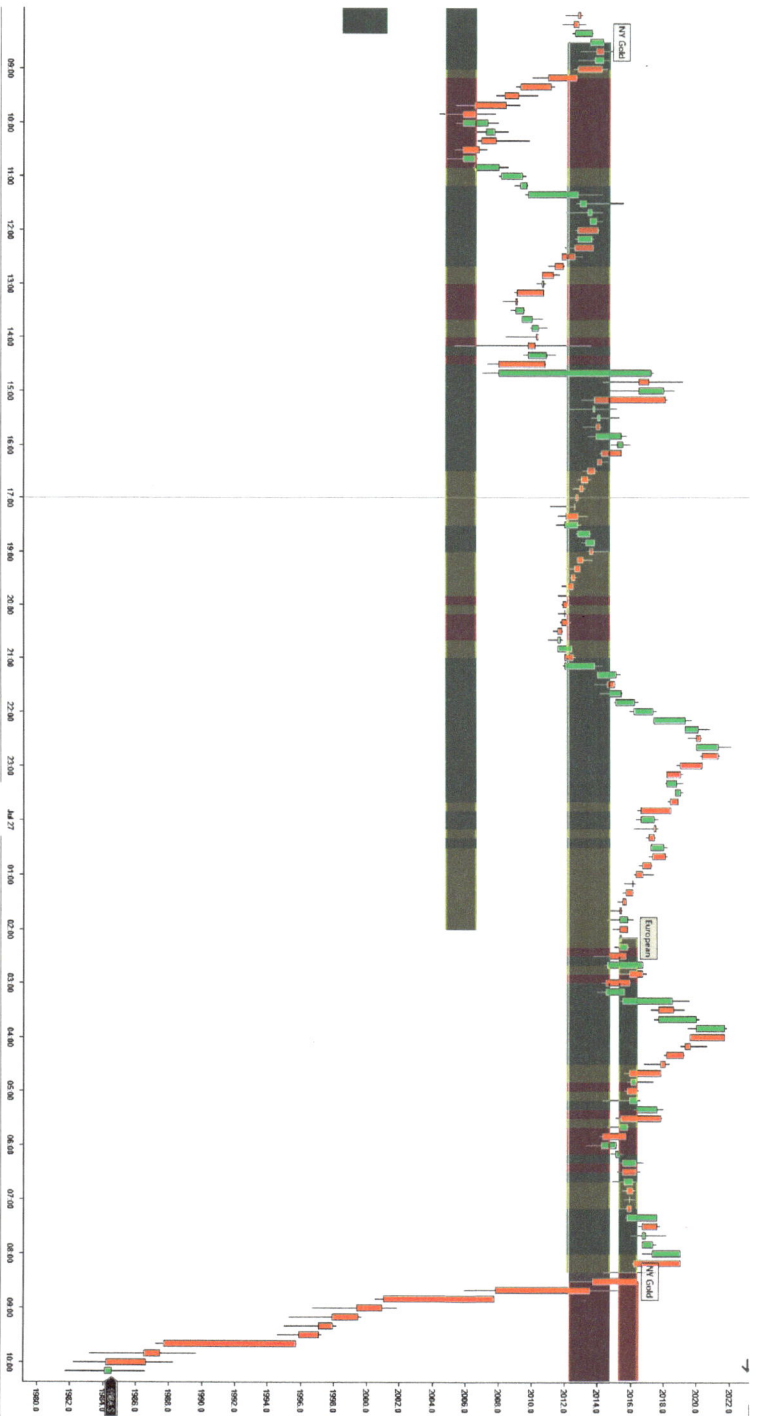

Chart 6.4 – Gold Futures Breakout with Economic Data.

show short-term support and resistance. Traders then employ different strategies to trade up and down within that range to make the most out of the trading opportunities.

This highly strategic and calculated approach to trading is a testament to the importance of understanding the intricacies of the market, as well as the factors that impact its movements. By keeping a close eye on opening ranges and other critical market events, traders can take advantage of price movements.

As we transition to the next day, market watchers are eagerly anticipating the arrival of significant economic data. The European opening range (labelled with a yellow background on the chart) is observed to have settled slightly above the previous day's New York gold pit opening range, creating a powerful confluence of ranges that typically serves as a robust support zone. Such price behaviour is relatively common in the lead-up to major economic announcements.

This confluence of ranges holds particular importance for traders seeking to make informed investment decisions. When both the European and New York markets align in this manner, it is often a strong indicator of potential market movements.

Then we get the New York gold pit open at 08:20 a.m., leading into the economic data point at 08:30 a.m. Traders have observed a confluence of the lower bound of this New York opening range to the previous day's lower bound, and they are unsure of the upcoming economic data. As a result, traders see the previous day's opening range low as support, and the BIAS of the range being defined is red. Consequently, traders are only looking for a short breakout and should be ready ten seconds or so before the opening range closes and the economic data is announced to put on their SHORT stop market order.

It's worth emphasizing that this economic data is a catalyst for large price movements most of the time, and traders must be ready to take advantage of these opportunities. In this case, the catalyst was a positive confluence of events. It sent the price action down in the same direction the BIAS of the opening range was indicating. As can be seen from the chart, the resulting trade was parabolic in nature as it broke down below the strong support offered by multiple lower bounds of opening ranges, and it offered traders some 280 ticks around 90 minutes. If a trader was trading one contract of gold futures, that would be a $2,800 trade.

PRICE DIRECTIONS

Now, let's look at another example, but this time, a bullish move after economic data. Once again, we will employ the same approach of analysing the preceding day's behaviour and the course of events leading up to the economic data.

Our attention is immediately drawn to the left side of Chart 6.5, as the New York gold pit opens just above the European gold pit open. It is worth noting that despite the opening range being colour-coded in red to indicate a short trade, the opportunity to execute such a trade is not present. This is primarily due to the fact that the European gold pit open acts as a reliable support, and it would only be wise to engage in a short trade if the price breaks below the European opening range. One more confluence was needed to trade, and it didn't happen!

Throughout the day, the price of gold futures remained trapped within a tight range, sandwiched between two

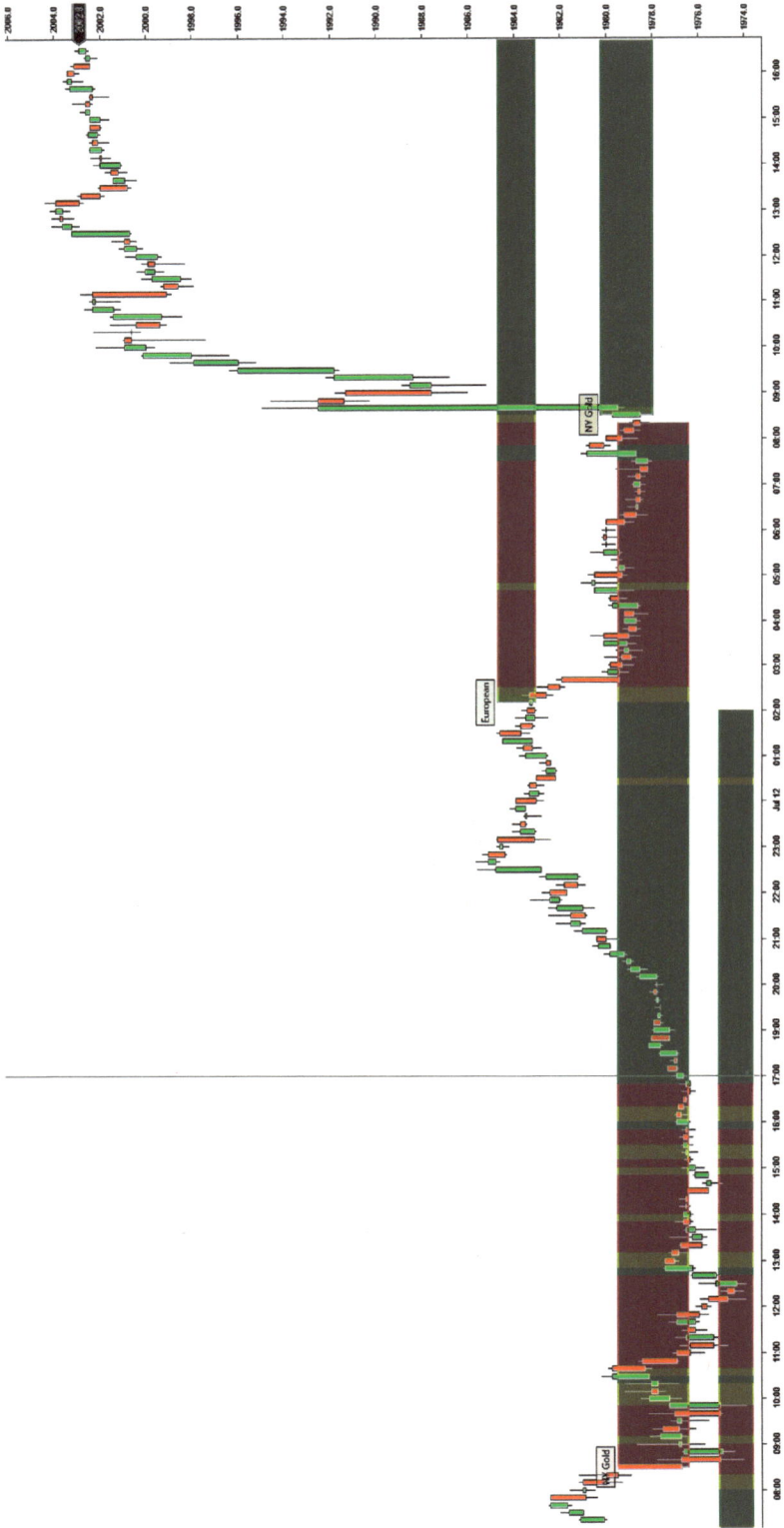

Chart 6.5 – Economic Data and Opening Ranges.

nearby opening ranges acting as both support and resistance levels. These confluences proved formidable, leaving little to no room for trading opportunities. The lack of volatility in the market presented a challenging environment for traders looking to profit from price movements. — a good reason not to trade gold futures on that day.

In the upcoming trading session, a beneficial opportunity is emerging for traders as the market is showing a clear move back up through the previous day's New York gold pit opening range. The bias of the range appears to be turning green. Additionally, there are multiple confluences of support and resistance present, including "fresh air" above (the space between the support and resistance zones that offers a lucrative trade opportunity with a decent risk-to-reward ratio) and ample time before the European gold pit opens.

By carefully analysing the market conditions, traders can see that the steady move up through the previous day's range indicates strength in the market. With all these factors considered, this presents a great chance to enter a long trade before the European gold pit opens.

However, traders must be cautious and remain aware of the timing of the European open as they must exit their long trade before then. The unknown volatility that could arise with the European gold pit open makes it critical for traders to remain vigilant and manage their trades accordingly.

Now, the European gold pit opens, and it's a data release day. Notice how the European gold pit opening range is coloured yellow, which means total indecision and a neutral BIAS. I chose this scenario as I wanted to touch on neutral BIAS and the specific trading opportunities it presents.

When approaching the markets with a neutral BIAS, a straddle-type entry strategy can be highly effective. This involves placing a stop market buy order just one tick above the range and also a stop market sell order just one tick below the range. By doing this, you can take advantage of the total indecision that often occurs during the opening range of a price movement.

One particularly intriguing confluence to note is the prevalence of spinning top candles in these opening ranges. These candles suggest that the highs of the opening range were soundly rejected and that the most likely order to take would be short. In fact, as evidenced by the chart, this was precisely what occurred — a short order was taken in. At this stage, the long order should be cancelled, and a stop loss for the short trade placed one tick above the high of the range.

It's worth noting that the upper bound of the previous day's New York gold pit opening range represents a sensible target. This is by no means a coincidence, as the price has a tendency to find support at this level. As a trader, keeping this information in mind can prove highly valuable when gauging the future direction of a price movement.

Now, going into the economic data point, we can observe that the New York gold pit opening range is currently displaying a yellow, neutral BIAS. Considering this information, it is imperative to implement the straddle-type entry strategy, which was elaborated upon previously. It is crucial to bear in mind that an explosive reaction to the data is what we are seeking. Consequently, traders must consider augmenting their long position by placing a stop market buy order for additional contracts above the high of the European opening range — just in case the reaction to the economic data is positive, and the price rises quickly.

Examining Chart 6.5, we can observe that the reaction was, indeed, explosive as the long order was executed, surpassing the New York gold pit open and subsequently smashing through the European gold pit open, further bolstering the long trade.

TAKEAWAYS

This trading strategy highlights the significance of identifying the confluences of support and resistance provided by opening ranges to make informed decisions and by maximising opportunities. Traders must not overlook the significance of confluences of support and resistance levels when it comes to economic data points and gold pit opens. However, these are not the only factors that can impact trading outcomes.

FED SPEECHES

Traders must also pay close attention to the speeches of different Regional Federal Reserve Bank presidents, which typically occur at 11 a.m. EST. This unique confluence of time and earlier opening ranges can have a substantial impact on the market, and failing to acknowledge this could result in missed opportunities for traders.

While not a daily occurrence, it is essential for traders to stay up to date on economic calendars so they are well-prepared when these speeches occur. Although some speeches may not cause any substantial movement in the market, traders need to be alert and watch closely for scenarios and orders that could be traded if the Regional Fed president says something that causes the US dollar to move. In other words, traders must carefully monitor price action compared to recent opening ranges and take into consideration the potential impact of Regional Fed speeches.

It's worth recalling our earlier discussion in the book about correlations because traders must recognize the relationship between the statements and speeches of Regional Fed presidents and market reactions. Notably, these reactions can directly affect the US dollar and indirectly influence gold prices through these correlations. As such, to succeed in the trading world, traders should be well-versed in not only economic data and gold pit open schedules but also Regional Fed speeches.

When it comes to speeches delivered by Fed presidents, traders need to exercise patience as they can sometimes be long-winded. Nonetheless, this presents an opportunity to strategize appropriately. In analysing Chart 6.6, traders can observe that the New York gold pit opening range falls within the boundaries of the earlier European gold pit opening range. This convergence marks the formation of both strong support and resistance levels. Given this setup, a considerable shift in the US dollar would require a remarkable statement from the Regional Fed president or another high-impact factor.

For context, the speech had been going for approximately twenty minutes, and at this point, the price action was below the confluence of opening ranges. In fact, even when the spinning top Doji candle attempted to test this area from below at 11:20 a.m., the highs were firmly rejected, further solidifying the dominance of the resistance and support levels.

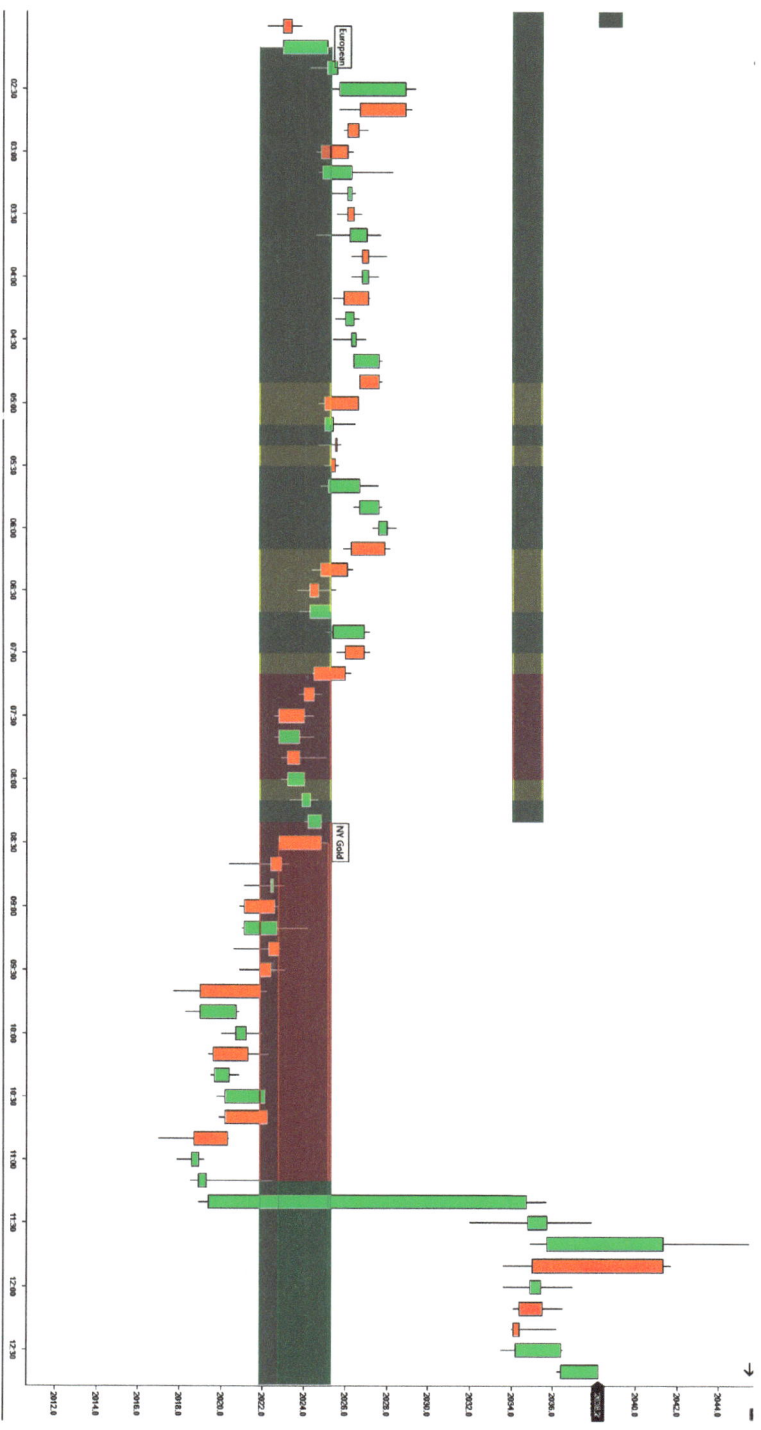

Chart 6.6 – Continuation Trading Range Breakouts.

At this point, however, the BIAS of the opening ranges turns green. When the BIAS turns green, it is indicative of a favourable environment for buyers, enabling attentive traders to recognize an opportunity for a stop market buy order. By strategically placing their orders above the highest point of these opening ranges, traders can capitalize on the impending price action if it occurs.

It is worth noting that the subsequent parabolic move upward that occurs approximately ten minutes later could not have been predicted. However, traders who possess a deep understanding of market behaviour and confluences would not be deterred by such unpredictability. Rather, they would leverage their knowledge to take full advantage of such situations.

TAKEAWAYS

On days of high economic data activity, traders must also pay attention to the data reactions and look for potential reversal trades. For instance, if the opening range of gold has a red bearish BIAS leading up to the data point, then a day trader would look for a long trade in the opposite direction of the BIAS.

It is crucial to note that these data reversal trades often happen dramatically, presenting an opportunity to make significant gains but also posing significant risks. Nonetheless, when the confluence of technical analysis and economic data release occurs, it can be a very powerful phenomenon that can provide tremendous value to traders and investors.

STRUCTURAL AND TECHNICAL STARTING STRATEGIES

Let us delve deeper into the analysis presented in chapter 5, where we explore the importance of Technical Starting Strategies. In Chart 6.7, we notice a strong linear support and resistance zone marked in blue, which stands out as a significant aspect across multiple timeframes.

As we examine the chart, we witness a straddle trade that shorted from the European gold pit open, reaching this particular zone as support. Interestingly, the bearish move witnessed a halt right at this juncture, once again confirming strong support. Subsequently, when the New York gold pit open tested this support, we observed that the BIAS for the opening range was red. In this scenario, traders had to be conscious of the combination of the potent support intertwined with impending economic data, creating the ideal circumstances for a data reversal trade that went contrary to the BIAS.

The reaction of the market to this situation was monumental, and the price sprang up in the blink of an eye. This example underscores the importance of paying attention to confluences of support and resistance with economic data points.

TARGET PRICES

This move was quick, which is challenging for traders because they need to plan targets and maybe even add to the trade. When a sudden uptick is observed, traders must act quickly and strategically to capitalize on the moment. In

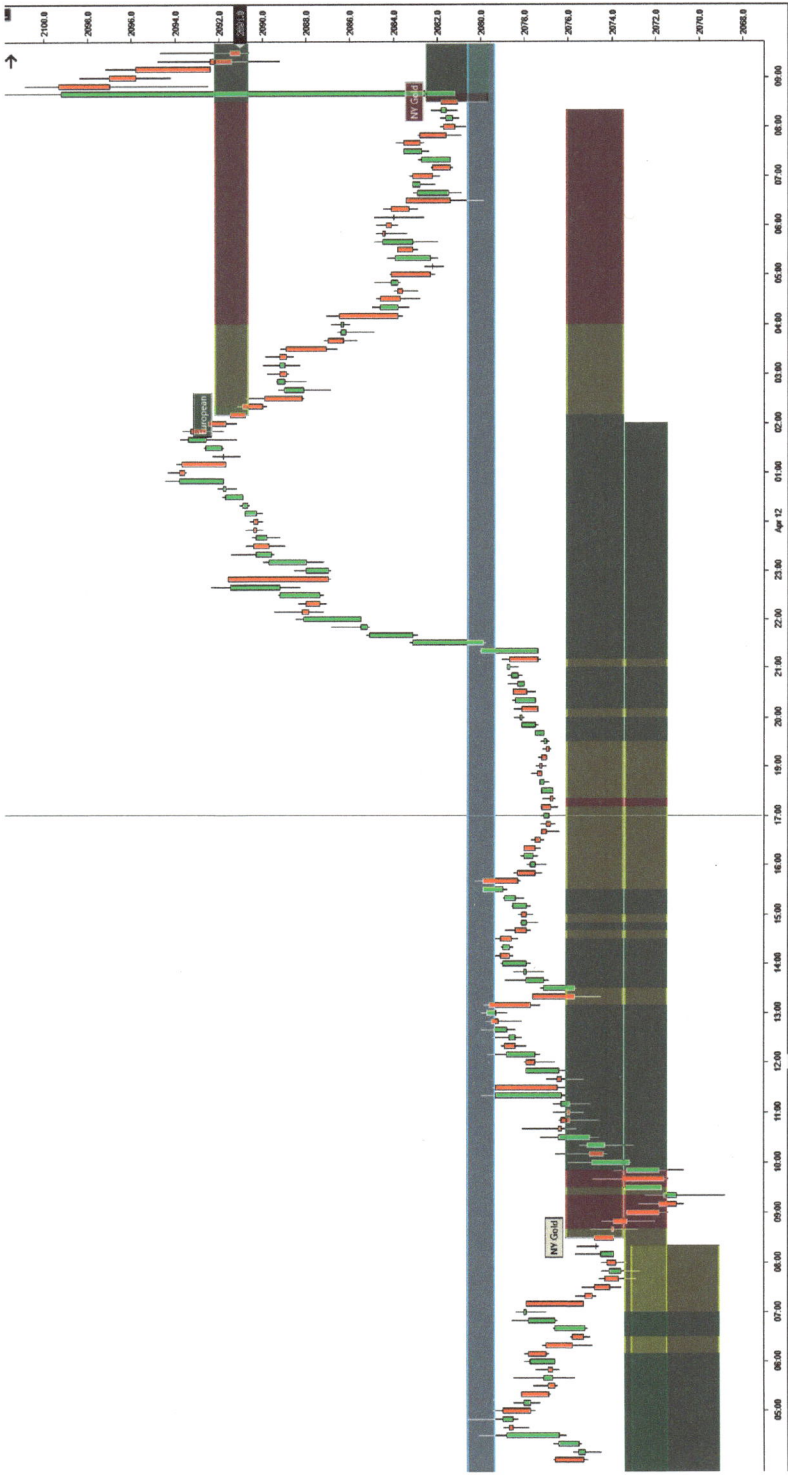

Chart 6.7 – Opening Range Breakout Trading with Structural Support and Reversals.

such instances, strategizing target prices and even considering adding to the trade become crucial.

One strong and relatively low-risk technique is to set the target at the European opening range, which would have yielded profits of over $1,000 per single traded contract in under ten minutes. While it's true that the price did break through the range soon after, it's worth noting that it retraced and was tested again at the far-right end of the chart. This observation shows that utilizing support and resistance levels is a reliable long-term strategy that seasoned traders appreciate.

Choosing ideal targets can be a tricky business. More experienced traders sometimes seek more out of their trades and might have expanded their scope. However, the safest solution is often the simplest one. In this case, setting the target at the European opening range would be a conservative yet fruitful strategy worth considering during similar market conditions.

STRUCTURAL SUPPORT AND RESISTANCE ZONES

A closer exploration of these structural support and resistance zones on multiple timeframes and their confluences will finish off our gold futures day trading journey for the range breakout strategy.

On Charts 6.8 and 6.9, the focus will be on the European gold pit open in the middle of the chart. The first of the charts has the 10-minute support and resistance zones coloured in yellow and the 15-minute support and resistance

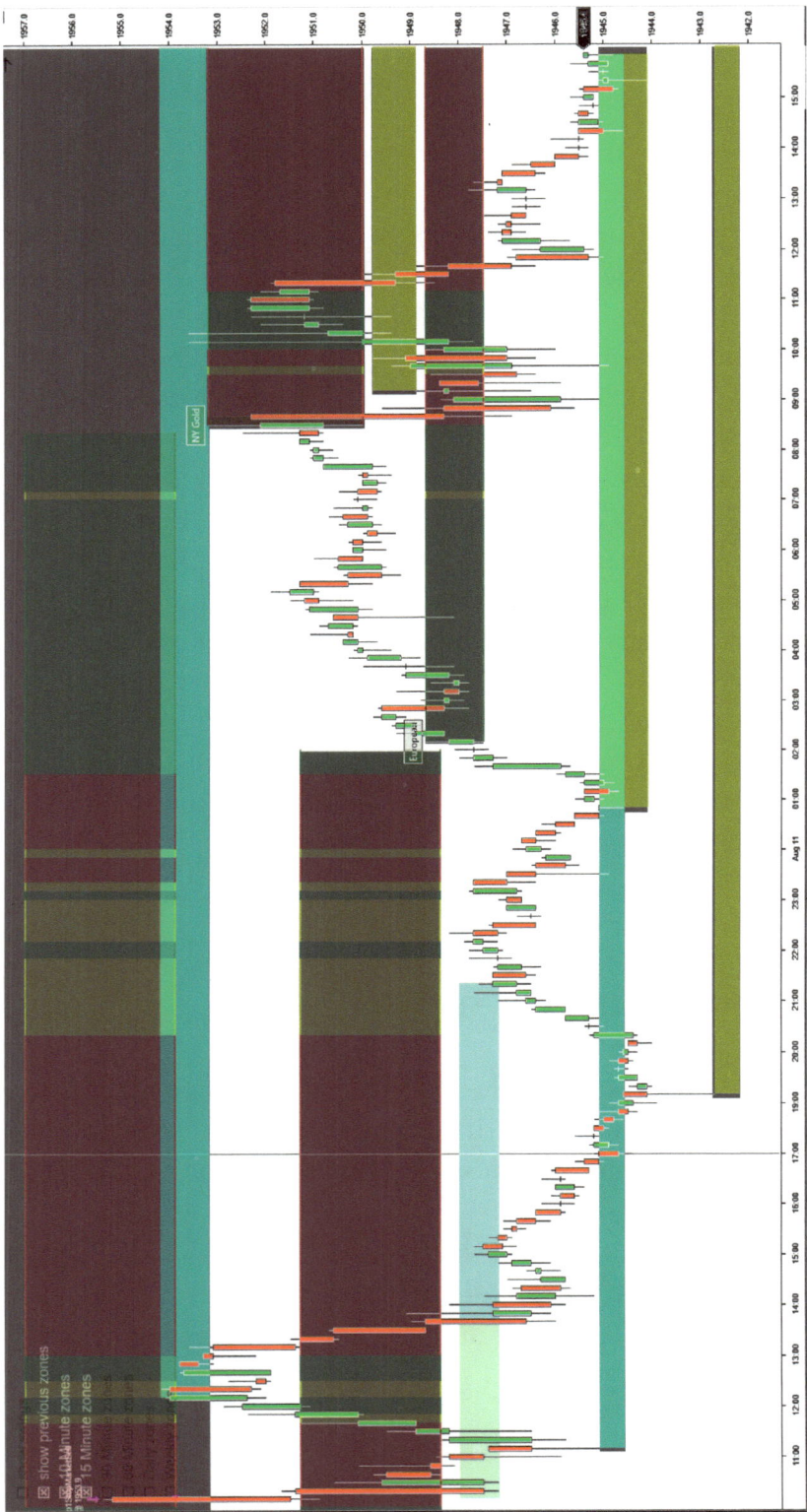

Chart 6.8 – Gold Futures Range Breakout Chart with 10- And 15-Minute Support and Resistance Zones Added.

zones in cyan. Note the confluence of 10- and 15-minute support and resistance zones between $1,944 and $1,946. The move from this support into the European open was strong, with lots of "fresh air" (the space between the support and resistance zones) up above until the next 15-minute resistance zone.

On Chart 6.9, the 30-minute support and resistance zones are added in green. Pay particular attention now to the European gold pit opening range lower bound finding support in this 30-minute support zone. Yet another confluence to support the green BIAS of the opening range and the bullish breakout trade. It is no coincidence that when we get the New York gold pit opening range, followed by economic data and the confluence of the 15- and 30-minute resistance zones, the price goes down from there. Confluences in resistance, opening range, and economic data create another "perfect storm."

TAKEAWAYS

Trading gold futures requires a thorough understanding of various technical indicators, market behaviour, volume, and economic data points. Traders must be vigilant during the European and US gold pit opening times, monitoring for breakouts of the initial trading range produced to predict potential future trends. By keeping up to date with the latest market trends and economic data releases, traders can develop a sound trading strategy led by confluences and make informed decisions that result in profitable trades.

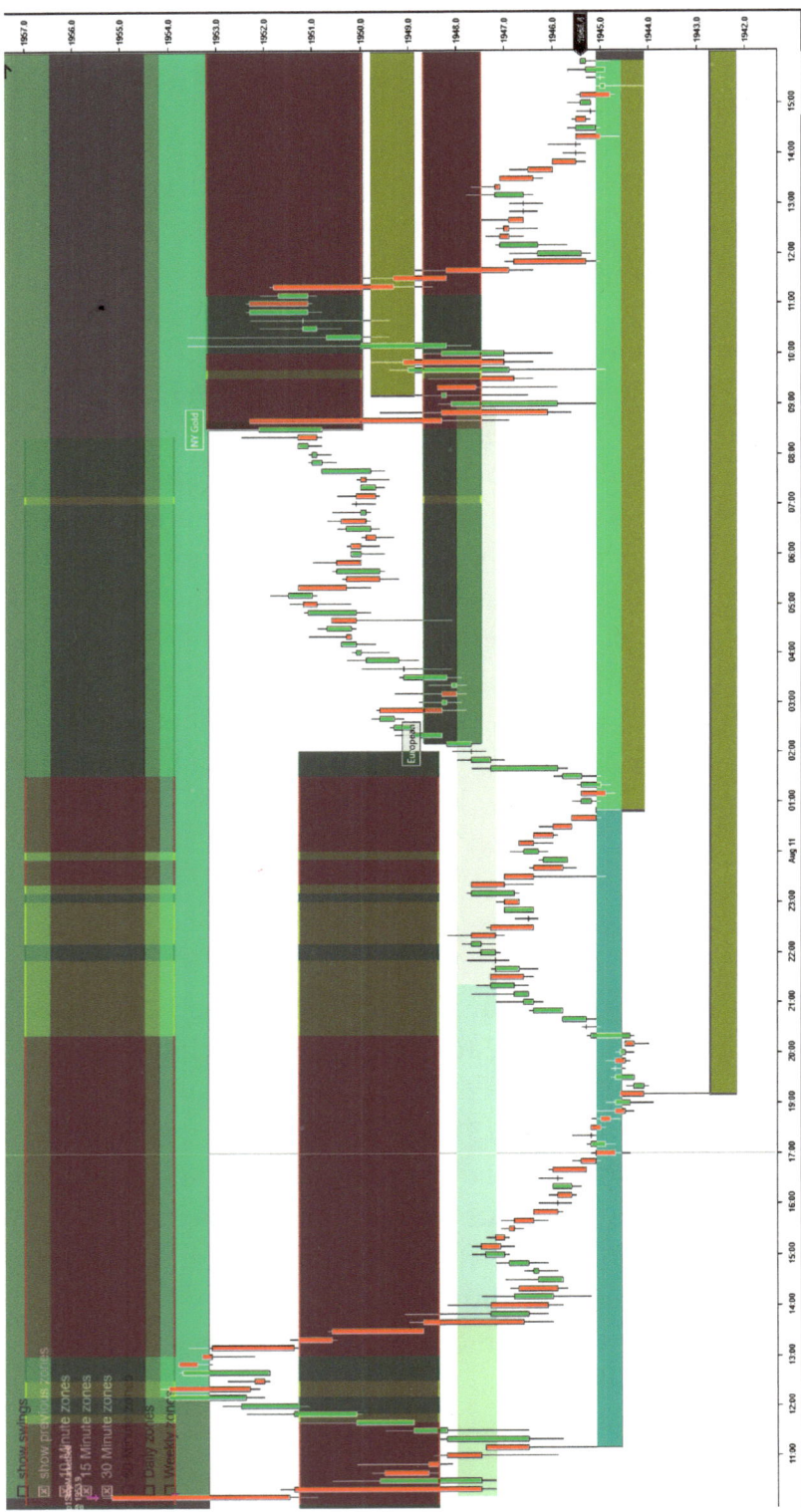

Chart 6.9 – Gold Futures Chart Continued with 30-Minute Support and Resistance Zones Added.

SOYBEAN FUTURES – $ZS

You may be asking yourself, what is this guy talking about here? Is he crazy? I had never thought of trading soybean futures, and these were my first thoughts, too, when one of our long-term software users introduced the idea to me with regard to our pullback strategy. I must say, before I even did the fundamental research, I checked out the charts and was blown away by the potential. I will let you be the judge when you have read through this section and walked through the chart example.

BACKGROUND

The global production of soybeans has increased significantly over the last seven years. In 2016, the worldwide production of soybeans amounted to approximately 337 million tonnes, whereas in 2020, it increased to about 360 million tonnes. Some groups estimate that world soybean production in 2022 and 2023 will be more than 390 million metric tons!

The rise in production can be linked to the growing demand for plant-based proteins, especially in developing countries. The top producers of soybeans in the world are the United States, Brazil, and Argentina, accounting for over 80 percent of the world's soybean production.

Over the past three years, the price of soybeans has been influenced by several events, including trade tensions, weather conditions, and the COVID-19 pandemic.

One of the most significant factors affecting soybean prices has been the ongoing trade war between the United

States and China. In 2018, the United States imposed tariffs on various Chinese goods, prompting China to retaliate with tariffs of their own. This led to a decline in demand for US soybeans, as China previously accounted for over 60 percent of US soybean exports. As a result, soybean prices fell to their lowest level in a decade.

In addition to the trade war, weather conditions have also impacted soybean prices. In 2019, heavy rainfall and flooding in the Midwest caused planting delays and reduced crop yields, leading to higher prices. The following year, drought conditions in South America, a major soybean producer, led to a reduction in production and higher prices.

Finally, the COVID-19 pandemic had a significant impact on global soybean prices. As the pandemic swept across the world, lockdowns and travel restrictions disrupted supply chains and reduced demand for soybeans. In particular, the closure of restaurants and other food service businesses led to a decline in demand for soybean oil, a key use for the crop.

CONFLUENCE FACTORS

As we can see, there are major confluences at play here. The increasing demand for soybeans is driving high volumes of trading in the futures market. As a futures day trader, it is critical to remember that we have the leeway to trade on whether the price goes up or down, provided we have the required volume and volatility for trading.

These confluences are creating an ideal trading environment, presenting lucrative opportunities for futures traders to make informed investment decisions. However, leveraging these opportunities requires a keen understanding of soybean market dynamics in terms of its supply and demand as well as the global events that impact its price fluctuation.

It is also important to stay informed on the latest developments and trends, such as South American weather patterns, shipping delays, and geopolitical tensions. All these factors impact the soybean futures market and must be carefully monitored to make strategic trading decisions.

US economic data has very little effect on Soybean prices, so the previous strategy that discussed large reactions to economic data with gold is moot with this instrument. This means that different types of day trading strategies need to be employed. The basic framing of charts with linear and non-linear support and resistance still holds strong, as it should with any financial instrument.

PULLBACK STRATEGY

This is where I want to bring in the concept of pullbacks during a directional move of a futures contract, as well as how to measure it and how to trade it. For instance, during a bullish move in soybean futures, some traders will opt to liquidate their positions in order to take profits. This selling pressure can induce a temporary reverse trend, causing the price to retrace slightly until more traders recognise the value and start buying again. The subsequent influx of buying interest can lead to a resumption of the prior bullish trend, potentially pushing the price even higher.

This dynamic is an example of how behavioural confluences allow the market to self-correct, balancing buying and selling pressures to find an equilibrium price. Market participants often study these patterns in order to identify potential buying and selling opportunities based on past trends and behaviour.

This type of strategy lends itself to using the UniRenko chart. This type of chart reduces the noise of insignificant price fluctuations, which means the pullbacks we see are significant and measurable.

FIBONACCI RETRACEMENTS AND EXTENSIONS

We use a combination of Fibonacci retracements to measure these pullbacks and Fibonacci extensions to determine targets for the next move in the direction of the main trend. I'm not going to delve too deep here, as we have software that does all this heavy lifting and calculating for us. So, I'm just going to brush over the basics.

Firstly, Fibonacci retracements are a popular technical analysis tool used by traders and investors in financial markets to identify potential levels of support and resistance. They are based on the mathematical principles of the Fibonacci sequence, which is a series of numbers in which each number is the sum of the two preceding numbers.

The most commonly used Fibonacci retracement levels are 23.6%, 38.2%, 50%, 61.8%, and 78.6%. These levels represent the percentage that an instrument has retraced from its previous move.

Fibonacci extensions are an important tool commonly used in financial markets to determine potential price targets. Essentially, these extensions are a continuation of the principles of the previously mentioned Fibonacci retracement levels, which are a series of ratios used to identify potential levels of support and resistance. While Fibonacci retracements tend to be used to identify potential price levels based on past movements, the extensions are forward-looking and are used to project potential future price levels.

The most common Fibonacci ratios used in determining price targets are 38.2%, 50%, 61.8%, 100%, 161.8%, and 261.8%. If the price continues to move in the direction of the existing trend, the extension levels can provide an estimation of where it may move next. The 100% extension, for example, suggests that the price will move to a level equal to the distance from the low to the high.

Confluences in Fibonacci measurements refer to the instances where two or more Fibonacci levels align closely with one another, giving a higher level of significance to a particular price level. These confluences are crucial as they signify potential turning points in the market where traders might enter or exit a position.

There are various factors that traders consider while identifying the confluences. For example, they may look at the clusters created by the intersection of the Fibonacci retracement levels with other technical indicators, such as moving averages, price support, and resistance levels. In addition, traders also look for confluences between Fibonacci retracements and extensions where the price retraces back to a Fibonacci level before continuing in the original trend or where the trend changes direction altogether.

But don't worry, there is software that can do this! It's just good to know the underlying concepts.

UNIRENKO CHART

Let's jump into an example with soybean futures on a UniRenko chart with the following settings:

- Tick Trend 1
- Open Offset 3
- Tick Reversal 5

These settings refer to the following:

A **tick trend** is a setting within the UniRenko chart that is designed to help traders identify the overall trend of a market. This setting works by tracking the number of ticks that a market moves before reversing direction. By setting a specific tick trend value, traders can see a clear picture of whether a market is trending up or down and adjust their trading strategies accordingly.

Open offset is another important setting in the UniRenko chart, which determines the placement of the open position on the chart. Essentially, this setting allows traders to control how the chart looks when they first start tracking a specific market. By adjusting the open offset, traders can make sure that they are starting with the right data and focusing on the most important information.

Finally, **tick reversal** is a setting that helps traders identify potential reversal points in a trend. This setting works by tracking the number of ticks that a market moves in the opposite direction before continuing on its original trend. By setting a specific tick reversal value, traders can effectively identify potential turning points in a trend and adjust their trading accordingly.

SLINGSHOT STRATEGY

It takes time to adjust these settings on a UniRenko chart in order to find the groove for each instrument for a particular time of the day, but as you can see in Chart 6.10, these settings are currently in the groove for $ZS, soybean futures for this type of strategy.

I call this type of strategy a slingshot trading strategy, as I view pullbacks against the main trend that meet the Fibonacci criteria as pulling back on a slingshot bowstring. Then, when they release, the movement continues in the direction of the main trend with more momentum. I have called our software that handles this, the xBrat SlingShot.

There are three slingshot trades on Chart 6.10, and I want to talk through each one. First, note the BIAS Depth heatmap at the foot of the chart. We mentioned the heatmap during the gold futures example, and it's good to note that it's a necessary tool for confirmation on all trading strategies. Then, we have support and resistance zones for the native timeframe (UniRenko

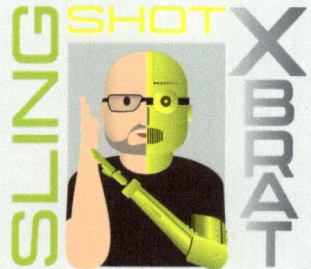

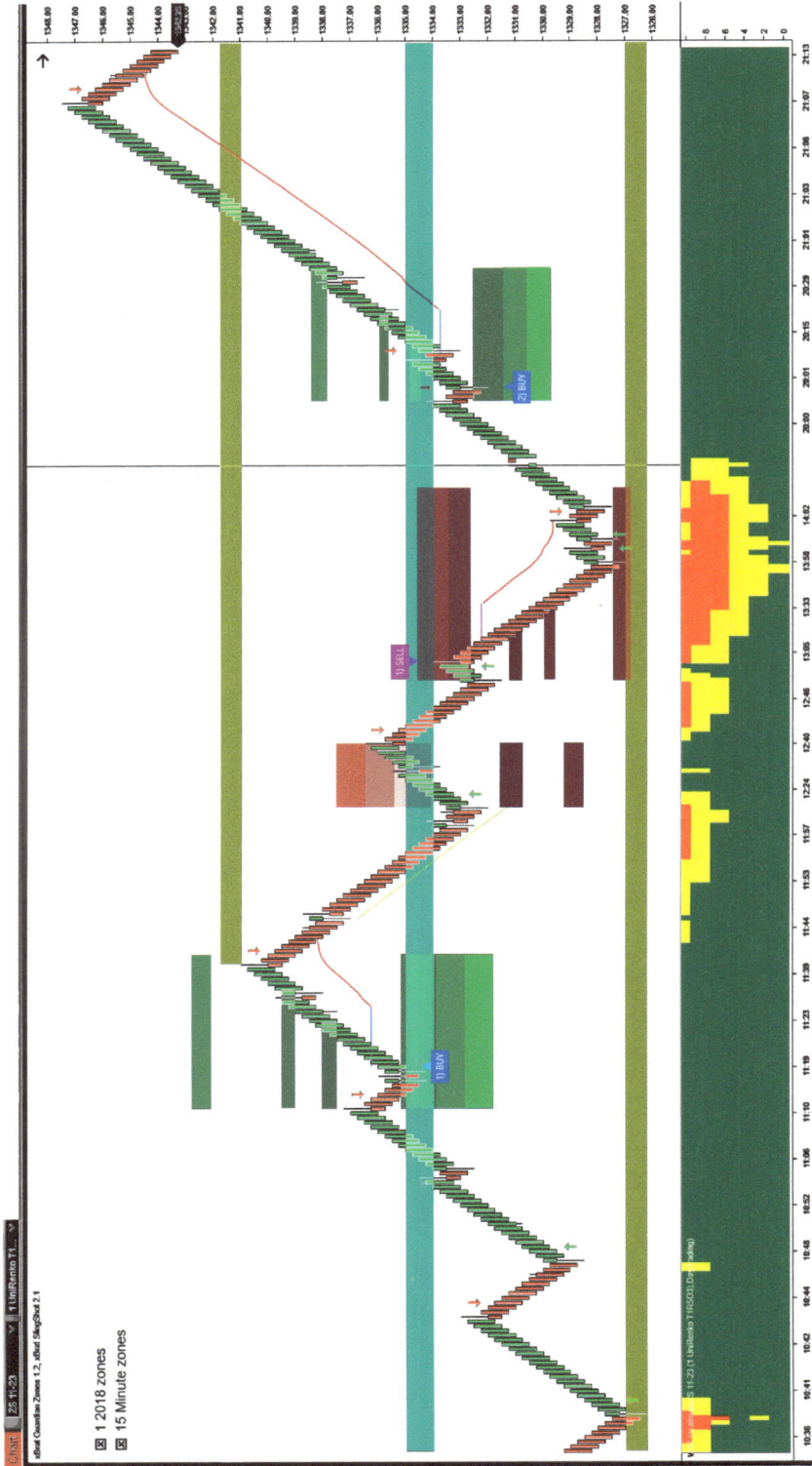

Chart 6.10 – Soybean Futures Unirenko Chart with Added Support and Resistance Zones and then Pullback Zones From Xbrat Slingshot Software.

1,3,5) in yellow on the chart and the 15-minute support and resistance zone in cyan on the chart. For this smaller time-frame, this is all we need for day trading soybean futures.

Let's start from the left on the chart to build the story. Price bounces off the yellow support zone and eventually pushes through the 15-minute resistance. Movement like this usually causes exhaustion and a profit taking pullback. The resulting pullback then found support at the 15-minute zone and also at the first of the three Fibonacci pullback zones of the SlingShot software. Also, all six timeframes on the BIAS Depth heatmap were green. A maximum of three out of three confluences with the tools being used cannot be ignored!

This first pullback zone represents an 85 percent proba-bility of the price slingshotting to target two. As can be seen on the chart, the price had its first wobble at target two with the first red UniRenko brick printed. It did continue to climb a little before reversing due to lots of profit taking. The red line on the chart that the price moves back down through is an EMA line used for trailing stop positions to reduce risk and lock in profit if traders don't take profits at targets. It is always prudent to have the safety of a trailing stop in all-day trading positions.

Next, the price action pushes just below the 15-minute support zone, then pulls back up into the middle of the pull-back zones, which represents an 80 percent probability of reaching target two. The software did not print a sell signal at this time as the logic in the algorithm was not met. The better trade, and hence the sell signal from the software, was when the price pushed down through the 15-minute support and then reversed to test the same zone as resistance. Then, the confluence of another pullback zone with this 15-minute resistance gave us two out of three as the BIAS Depth heatmap was mixed. Two out of three was a decent probability, as there was also confluence in the third target zone and the previous native timeframe support zone. This confluence for target was hit "to the tick" before reversing!

The last trade is interesting as the software gave an entry below the 15-minute resistance, where any sensible trader would put their stop market buy order just one tick above this zone for safety. The software has rules to follow for these very shallow pullbacks and is aggressive with entries.

But as far as the behaviour is concerned, it was a textbook move up from previous support to test the 15-minute resistance zone, which caused a slight pullback into the first of the three pullback zones, giving an 85 percent probability of the price reaching target two. Once the price broke through the 15-minute zone, it flew. This is why we also employ EMA's as trailing stops. It allows us to catch those runners that fly through the normal Fibonacci extension target zones due to increased momentum from the slingshot effect of the pullback and traders seeing value.

I mentioned percentage probabilities to hit target two in this section and want to briefly explain this. In basic terms, confluences of both Fibonacci retracements and extensions form very strong technical zones. The measurements used in both are incorporated into the SlingShot software and allow us to identify the sweet spot for each. This allows us to put a confident percentage probability figure to these relationships of pullback zones to target two. But not forgetting the last trade, these can be smashed through, and we must be ready for this with an EMA trailing stop.

TAKEAWAYS

Soybean futures are not commonly traded by retail traders at the moment, but institutional traders are indeed taking advantage of the confluences that drive price fluctuations in this instrument. In time, I believe, more retail traders will jump onto this and make soybean futures their go-to instrument for trading. There are other types of strategies that use volume that are also very strong for soybean futures, but I want to use a different instrument next to discuss this day trading strategy and its confluences.

OIL FUTURES – $CL

Oil futures are one of the main futures contracts traded by day traders around the world, as they are highly liquid. Consequently, there is always a large pool of active buyers and sellers in the market. The high level of liquidity of oil futures translates to tighter bid-ask spreads, lower transaction costs, and faster execution times compared to less liquid assets.

Oil futures trading is heavily influenced by political and economic events, such as geopolitical tensions, economic growth, and supply and demand factors. Consequently, astute traders need to stay abreast of global developments and confluences to develop informed trading strategies and minimize risks.

Successful oil futures trading requires a deep understanding of technical analysis, as well as fundamental factors that determine oil prices. By analysing historical price patterns, market trends, and other indicators, traders can make informed decisions about when to enter and exit positions.

Although the Chicago Mercantile Exchange (CME) trading floor does not have a physical oil pit anymore, there is still increased activity at the notional oil pit open at 9 a.m. EST each trading day. The opening range breakout strategy is, therefore, relevant to trading oil, but we don't have any economic data around this open like we do for gold, so reversals are off the strategy table. Traders must also consider that there is only one opening range each day, unlike gold futures, which have both a US and European open. So, we need to combine two or more trading strategies and look for confluences to be more consistent with trading oil futures. I now want to introduce VWAP.

VOLUME-WEIGHTED AVERAGE PRICE (VWAP)

For day traders, understanding the volume-weighted average price (VWAP) is essential in developing a successful trading strategy. VWAP is a crucial indicator for measuring the average price of a security during a given trading day, taking into account both volume and price levels. This formula is especially useful for traders who require insight into market trends and the best times to buy or sell.

The VWAP calculation is determined by multiplying the price of each transaction by its corresponding volume and then taking the sum of all of these values. The resulting figure is divided by the total volume of all transactions during the day to derive an average price. This is known as the VWAP, which serves as the reference price for that day. On Chart 6.11, this is identified as the dotted line coloured cyan. The green and red dotted lines are Fibonacci extensions of the VWAP and form part of the logic of the xBrat VWAP Predator trading indicator strategy.

Where you see the blue buy signal candles is the other part of the logic, which looks for an open on one side of the VWAP or VWAP extension lines and a close on the other side. This candle also must have a higher than average volume and be an accumulation candle for buy signals or a distribution for sell signals. So, we have built in lots of technical confluences around volume for this strategy.

Next, I will talk about combining both the opening range breakout strategy with the VWAP Predator strategy.

OPENING RANGE BREAKOUT WITH THE VWAP PREDATOR STRATEGY

Again, let's walk through the behaviour from the left of the chart and discuss the confluences and

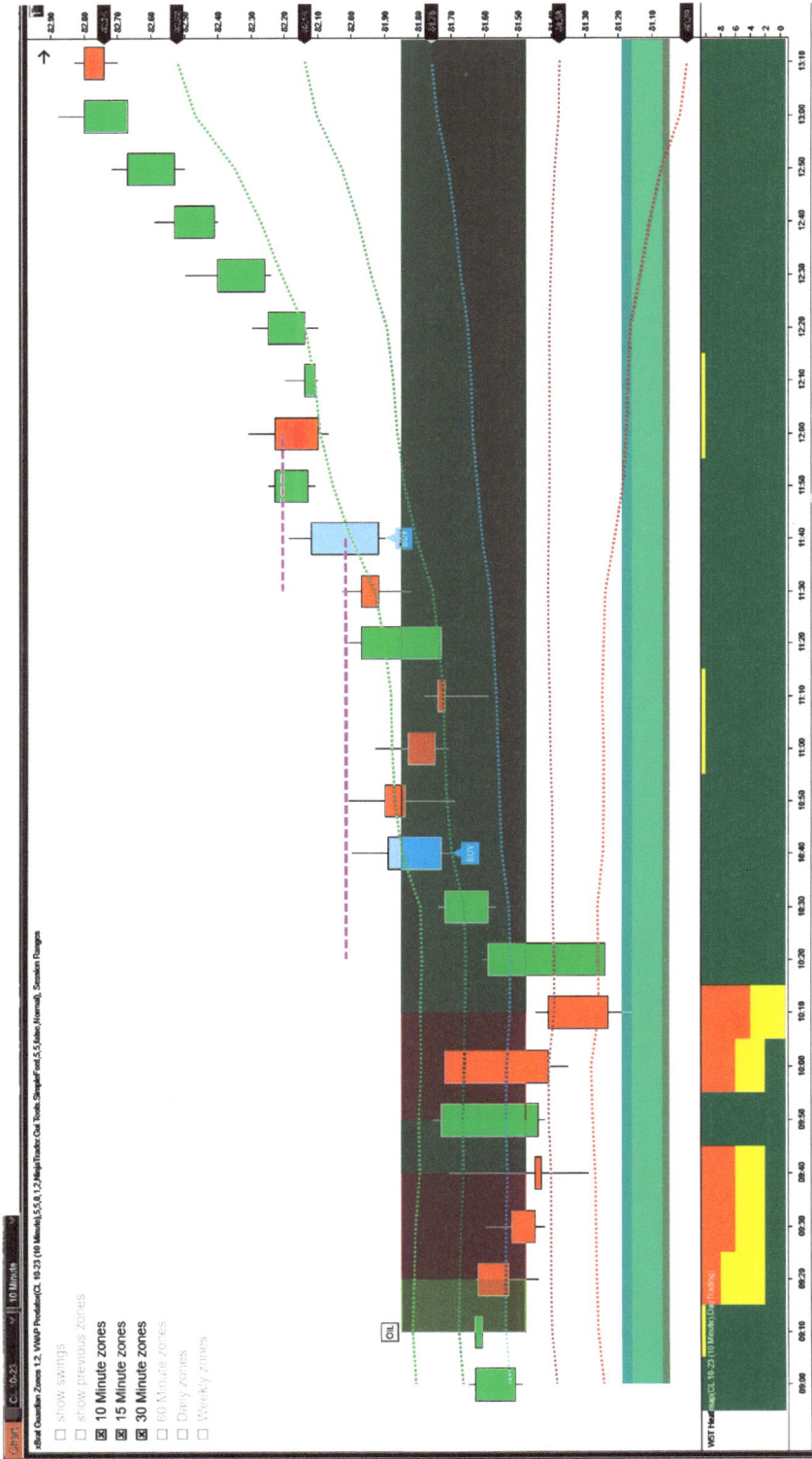

Chart 6.11 – Oil Futures Chart with VWAP Trading.

decisions to be made in this situation when day trading oil futures. The oil pit opening range is defined and coloured in yellow, which indicates indecision. As discussed with gold, this would usually be set up as a straddle entry; however, we have the confluence of the 15- and 30-minute support zones, so the short order is not put on by the trader — no fresh air, no trade! The long order for the straddle is not taken in within three candles (30 minutes) of the opening range, so that order is cancelled. Remember, traders are looking for a breakout with force quickly, and this did not happen.

The price did meander down to test the confluence support zone, found support, and moved back into the opening range. As it did so, the six timeframes on the BIAS Depth heatmap turned green, and the opening range turned green — an encouraging confluence of BIASes.

Then, at 10:40 a.m., as the price moved out of the range, we get our first VWAP predator buy signal. So now we have confluences in the BIAS and two different trading strategies — a perfect storm and time to take a long position. The stop market order is placed one tick above the high of the buy signal candle and, interestingly, didn't activate for some time. The long position was taken in just one candle before the next buy Signal.

The confluences of the BIAS are still strong, and momentum has given traders an opportunity to add to their position with this next buy signal, with entry at the magenta dashed line, one tick above the high of the second buy signal candle. And then the remainder of the chart shows the bullish move continuing for profitable trade.

TAKEAWAYS

Identifying these confluences requires discipline and patience. Traders must wait for the "stars to align" before taking any action. Doing so helps to ensure that the probability of success is greater. Traders must not feel the need or pressure to take trades and must have the ability to "sit on their hands" until the time is right.

The importance of confluences cannot be understated. By identifying these confluences, traders can significantly increase their chances of success while minimizing the risk of loss. This is because confluences are often indicative of a trend reversal or a significant price movement.

S&P500 FUTURES – $ES

I couldn't finish a day trading chapter without working through the S&P500 ($ES) futures. The S&P500 index is a commonly used gauge of the US stock market, representing the top 500 publicly traded companies in the country. It is a market-weighted index, which means that the larger companies have a greater impact on its value. The index is widely used by investors as a benchmark for stock market performance, and its movements are closely watched and analysed by financial experts.

The liquidity of the S&P500 index and the futures contracts associated with it is high, making it attractive to investors looking for a market that is easily traded. This liquidity is due in part to the size and popularity of the index, as well as the large number of companies represented in it. Additionally, the futures contracts associated with the S&P500 index are among the most widely traded derivatives in the world.

REDUCING RISK

I do not really need to say too much more except how to day trade whilst reducing risk. This time, I'm going to introduce a multiple timeframe strategy alongside two signal trading strategies, building confluences even more into trading the futures contract with the most liquidity.

Chart 6.12 illustrates the 15-minute timeframe that is used for the opening range breakout strategy with $ES. There is a lot going on here, so let's start at the NYSE opening range. The opening range formed just above a confluence of multiple 60-minute support zones (pink). So, although the range is coloured red, and we would usually look for a short trade breaking out the lower bound of the opening range, we stay out as the confluence support is too much.

See how the candle after the opening range rejected the lows at the confluence support and formed a hammer-type candle. A high-volume rejection of the lows at strong support is a sign that the price is going to move higher, but we don't have confirmation on this timeframe with this strategy. So, it is wise to move down to a smaller timeframe and look for confirmation from a different type of strategy to get the confidence of multi-timeframe and multi-strategy confluence. I will discuss this more using Chart 6.13.

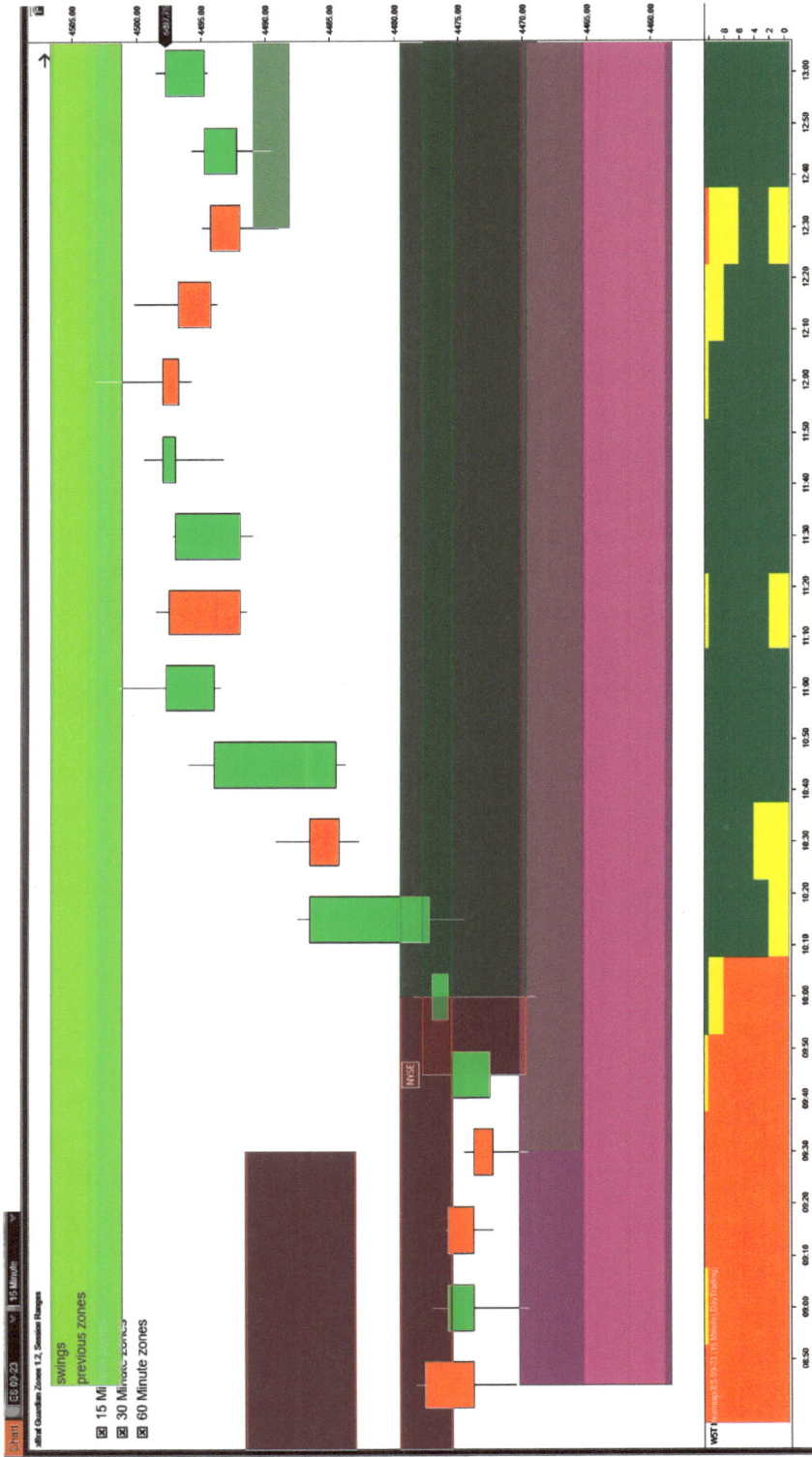

Chart 6.12 – S&P500 Futures Chart with Support and Resistance Zones Just Below the Opening Range.

On Chart 6.13, we're moving down to the 3-minute timeframe and introducing the xBratAlgo strategy. The xBratAlgo is a strategy that looks at the confluence of twelve points of control where, in this example, a 5* BUY is 11 out of 12, and a 6* BUY has 12 out of 12 confluences through these points of control.

The yellow down arrow on Chart 6.13 depicts the point where the first 15-minute candle closed on the higher timeframe, and the opening range was formed. Observe, just two candles later, the price testing of the confluence support zone mentioned earlier. The price then moves up from there. The first xBratAlgo Signal is a 5* BUY, but not all timeframes on the BIAS Depth heatmap are green, so we don't have all the confluences yet.

The next candle prints a 6* BUY, with all six timeframes green on the BIAS Depth heatmap. Furthermore, there is lots of fresh air to the next resistance zone, which is a confluence of the 3-minute and 15-minute resistance zones. The confluences are now strong across multiple timeframes on multiple strategies, BIAS Depth, and fresh air. It's a "perfect storm" that cannot be ignored, so traders should take the long position with a target of the confluence resistance zone above.

CONCLUSION

In conclusion, day trading futures requires traders to develop a comprehensive understanding of the confluences of geopolitical events, economic data, and fundamental drivers that can influence market prices. Combining

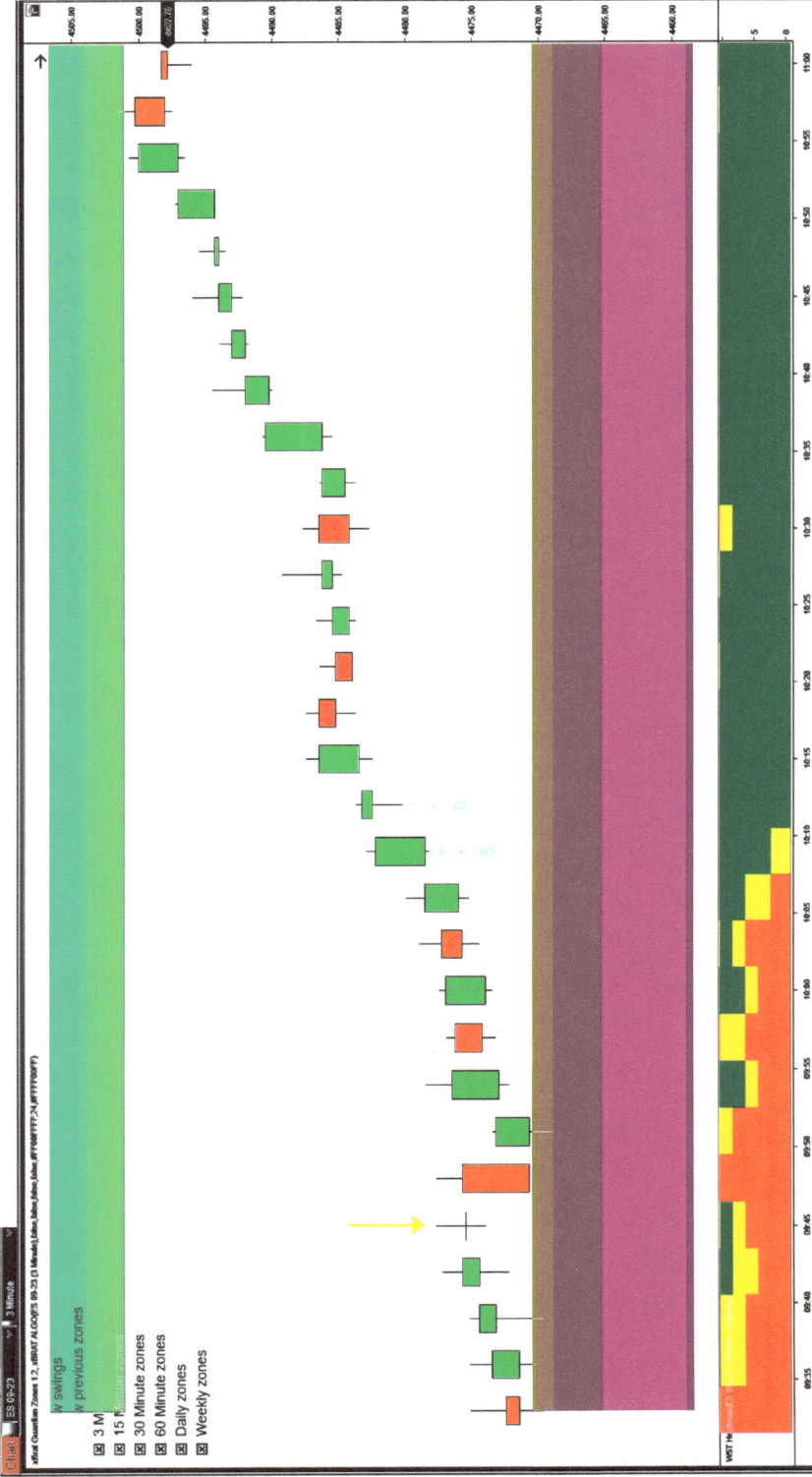

Chart 6.13 S&P500 – Chart with Same Support and Resistance but Not a Confluence of Technical Strategies.

technical analysis on the same and multiple timeframes can help traders identify patterns, trends, and key support and resistance levels. Successful futures traders use this combination of analysis to identify trading opportunities and reduce risks, making informed decisions that maximize their trading wins.

CHAPTER 7

Trend Behaviour

BEFORE WE MOVE on to swing trading and investing, I want to explain the concept of trend behaviour. After all, when we are swing trading or investing, we are looking for an instrument that is trending or, indeed, at the start of a trend reversal. Understanding this behaviour and then applying a confluence strategy can be very powerful.

But we need to walk before we can run. Remember back at the beginning of the book, where I mentioned my observations about the up and down flows when I first started trading? Over the years, I have taken this initial behavioural pattern and formalised it with rules that are simple and repeatable. Once learned, it will become second nature.

TREND BEHAVIOUR AND HERD MENTALITY

Has a parent or teacher ever asked you, "If your friends jump off a cliff, would you do it too?"

Of course not! That's insane. You're a strong and independent free thinker. Why would you do that? Herd mentality! You've certainly heard the term. It refers to the phenomenon where individuals adapt their views or opinions to conform to those of the group (or herd).

But what if your friends weren't jumping off a cliff?

Instead, what if they're all buying shares in the latest tech stock? Every day, you see the price going up a little. And your friends are talking about how great the tech company is.

After a while, it's not so much a question of *if* you're going to buy shares in this tech stock but *when* ...

"How does this help with a trading strategy?" you may ask.

Think of it this way. If you follow the herd mentality and buy the same stocks as your friends, it isn't likely to move the price. However, what about institutional traders? They are human beings, after all. Even the algo's were programmed by human beings!

You're probably thinking, "So what!"

Here's what often happens. When an institutional trader sees value in an instrument and buys a sizeable number of shares in that stock, then suddenly, other traders start to notice. After a quick analysis, they start to buy, which makes the price begin to move up. As momentum gathers and more traders join in (they don't want to be left out), the price trends even higher. This upward trend doesn't last forever since the human, institutional traders who got in early will eventually want to start taking profit. They do have their bonuses to think of, after all.

When some early buyers decide to sell their positions to take a profit, other institutional traders may join in to cover any major sell-offs and to bank some profit. At a certain price point, traders who joined the "herd" later may find themselves at a price point that's even lower than their original entry point.

This is a critical time in a trend! If the traders in slight loss-making positions still see strong growth potential in the instrument, then they're likely to buy more shares at a lower price, thus lowering their average holding price. Other traders may see this bullish volume and view this pullback as an opportunity to get in the bull herd.

Conversely, if the traders in slight loss-making positions start to panic when the selling volume increases, they're likely to sell their positions to reduce risk and loss. Some of the early entry traders who are still in the game may see this high bearish volume and decide to close the rest of their positions and take the remaining profit. Then, more traders sell and join the bear herd. In many of these scenarios, we see the bullish trend fail.

Allow me to share an intriguing story about a new herd of traders who have embraced our software. For the past couple of years, I have been emphasizing the significance of my focus on only day trading copper futures and the merits of day trading a singular instrument. Astonishingly, it appears that hundreds of these traders have now made the switch to trading copper futures!

This fascinating development has not only brought together a new herd of copper traders but has also contributed to their trading decisions. Now, this new herd of traders is not going to influence the price movements of copper futures very much, but they are influencing themselves by making better trade decisions. The herd is now trading more confidently and with a greater sense of control. This new-found confidence has enabled them to learn from each other's experiences and take note of past successes and failures.

What's particularly captivating is that it was a confluence of factors that led to this. These traders discovered our software, actively participated in our live webinars, and heeded my experience regarding copper futures and the importance of focusing on just one instrument. Their trading approach has undoubtedly undergone a transformation, and it offers an insightful example of how a shared vision can shape trading strategies.

TRENDS ON A CHART

A technical chart can tell the story of a stock's trend behaviour. I have found that a daily timeframe is the truest timeframe when swing trading a trend. You must think of each bar/candle as a measurement of a whole trading session. It has an open, a high, a low, and a close. Then, when you put all these daily bars together, you have a real picture of how this stock is performing and where it is in a trend (or if it is not in a trend). Chart 7.1 tells a trend story, and the short version of this story follows (remember, you can view a digital version by going to PaulBratby.com/Book-Club).

Let's start on the left of the chart with the low pivot around the end of 2020 after the COVID-19 pandemic pullback found its low. The move up from this low was reasonably parabolic in nature initially and was the start of a new bullish trend as stocks in the US recovered from the uncertainty of COVID-19.

PHASE 1 –
THE START OF POTENTIAL BULLISH TREND

As you can see in Chart 7.1, after the COVID-19 low, buying volume starts to pick up, and price action starts to move up. We get our first impulse move (1). Be under no illusions — this breakout, for the most part, needed a catalyst. The catalyst could be earnings, a news event specific to the company, or even a broader reaction within the sector where the stock resides. But, in this example, it was the realization that the world was not going to end due to COVID-19. In any case, brokers see this catalyst and try to stimulate this stock. They raise the price of the stock to see if any holders want to sell and, of course, if there are investors interested in buying.

You will notice the gap in price action during this first bullish impulse move (1). This was a reaction to good earnings. It means that, during the out-of-hours trading sessions (post- and pre-market), institutional traders were buying as many shares as they could get a hold of, even when brokers were increasing the price!

So, when the regular trading session started that day, the price was much higher than the previous day's close. This behaviour was another catalyst that continued the first bullish impulse move.

PHASE 2 –
THE FIRST REAL PROFIT TAKING PULLBACK

At this point, we get some profit taking (2). This is a natural reaction, especially from the investors who purchased shares

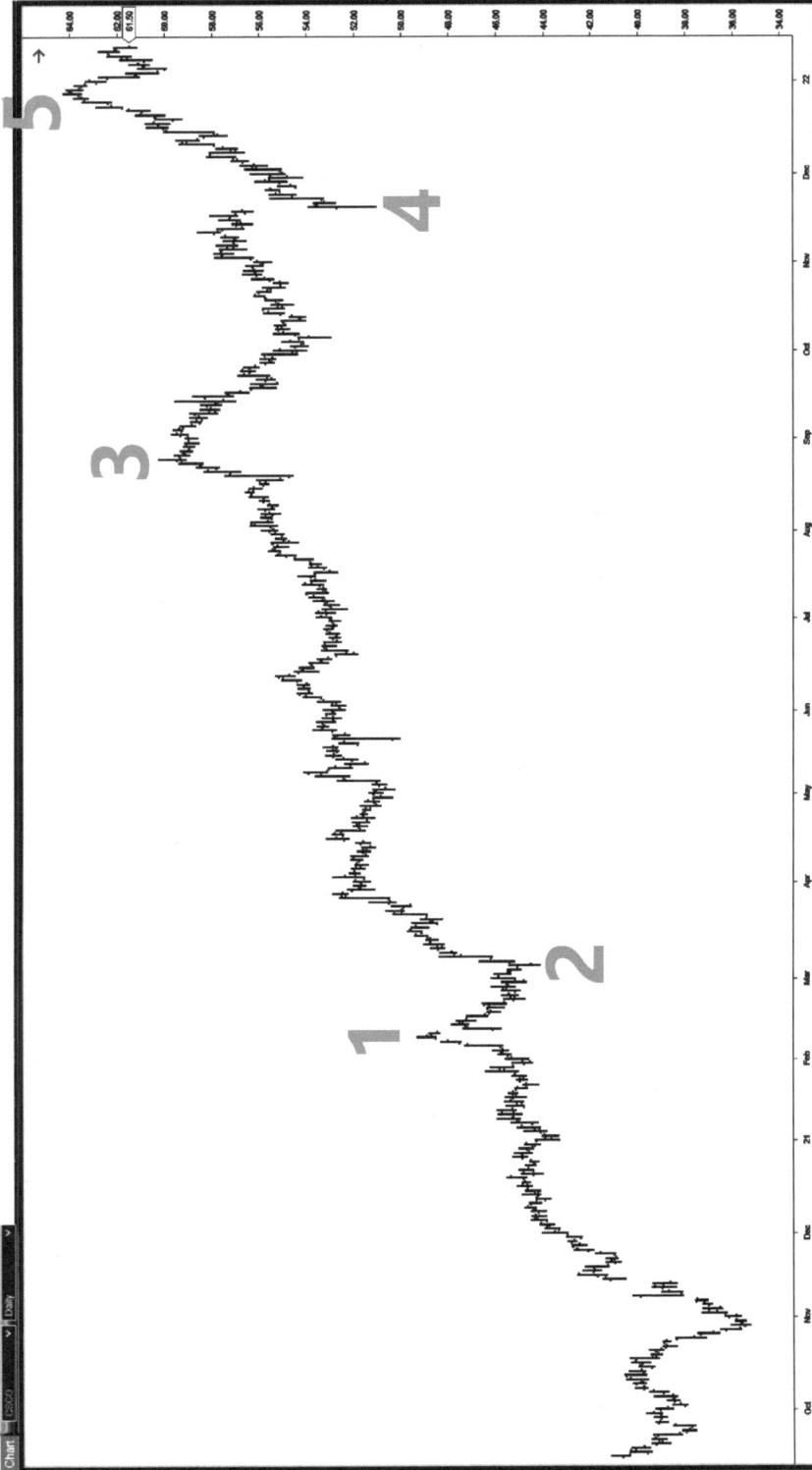

Chart 7.1 – Labelling Trend Behaviour.

during previous lows and even from those who purchased shares before the gap up after earnings. One important thing to note is that the volume would have been low during this pullback; hence, it is quite shallow with respect to the first impulse move (1).

PHASE 3 –
CRITICAL PHASE FOR THE BULLISH TREND

As I mentioned earlier, this next phase is a critical time for a potential long-term bullish trend. If those investors in slight loss-making positions still see value and start adding to their positions, then brokers will pounce and start raising the bid for the share price. Then, the next bullish impulse leg (3) will start with increasing volume. This third phase is usually longer in time and price action than the first phase. The pace generally picks up for the bullish move once the price breaks through the pivot high of the first bullish impulse move. This, for many traders, is a great time to add to or, indeed, start their position in this stock.

PHASE 4 –
NEXT PROFIT TAKING PULLBACK

Momentum and herd mentality have effectively driven the price up, but institutional traders will need to take profit at some stage. Herd mentality is still holding here, but at some point, a catalyst usually occurs and activates a behaviour change. The catalyst could be that the company is approaching its next earnings call, which may lead to traders protecting their profits by reducing position size. Or the catalyst could be a specific news event for the company or a swing in the sector where the stock resides. At this stage, we get our second and longer profit taking pullback (4). Again, note that normal behaviour here would see the volume reduce as we go deeper into the pullback.

PHASE 5 –
THE FINAL PUSH

Here, we get a high-volume rejection of the lows, a bullish signal, right at the low pivot (4) that starts the final bullish impulse move. Unsurprisingly, the herd turns right back around as institutional traders again see value after this low-volume profit taking pullback. And, of course, brokers pounce and test the waters with higher bid prices that are taken. A catalyst, again, will play a part in this behaviour. Maybe it's good earnings! This impulse move usually has less momentum than that in phase 3. Many institutional traders will take a lot of notice of the behaviour as the price moves through the high pivot formed on phase 3. They will tighten stops and may even take small profits to cover a potential correction. At this point, the bullish trend may run out of juice unless another good news catalyst gives a boost to momentum.

This is a very simple description of the behaviour presented by this stock. But keeping things simple is what traders need to do!

ADDING SUPPORT AND RESISTANCE

Now, let's add support and resistance zones and discuss confluences. Chart 7.2 is a daily chart on CSCO. The magenta support and resistance zones are for the weekly support and resistance zones, and the daily are in yellow. As the first bullish impulse move was approaching the weekly resistance zone (which actually was the zone of price prior to the pandemic pullback), CSCO announced earnings on 9 February 2021. The earnings data was reasonably good, but the confluence of the weekly resistance zone just up above, as well as uncertainty still surrounding COVID-19 and the strength of the worldwide recovery, was enough for some traders to take some profit. This is normal behaviour in a trend with so many confluences leading to decision-making!

Once the return to the bullish trend occurs, we see the price breaking through the weekly zone (just above the $50 price), which, for a great deal of traders, should have been the signal to buy more shares in CSCO. The earnings report on 18 May 2021 for CSCO (highlighted and zoomed in via the red arrow on the chart) had an initial gap down at the open into the weekly support zone, which was previously resistance. Immediately, traders found value at this price as we had a confluence of good earnings and the test of this crucial weekly support and resistance zone. This was enough to gather momentum for the largest yet bullish impulse move to pivot 3.

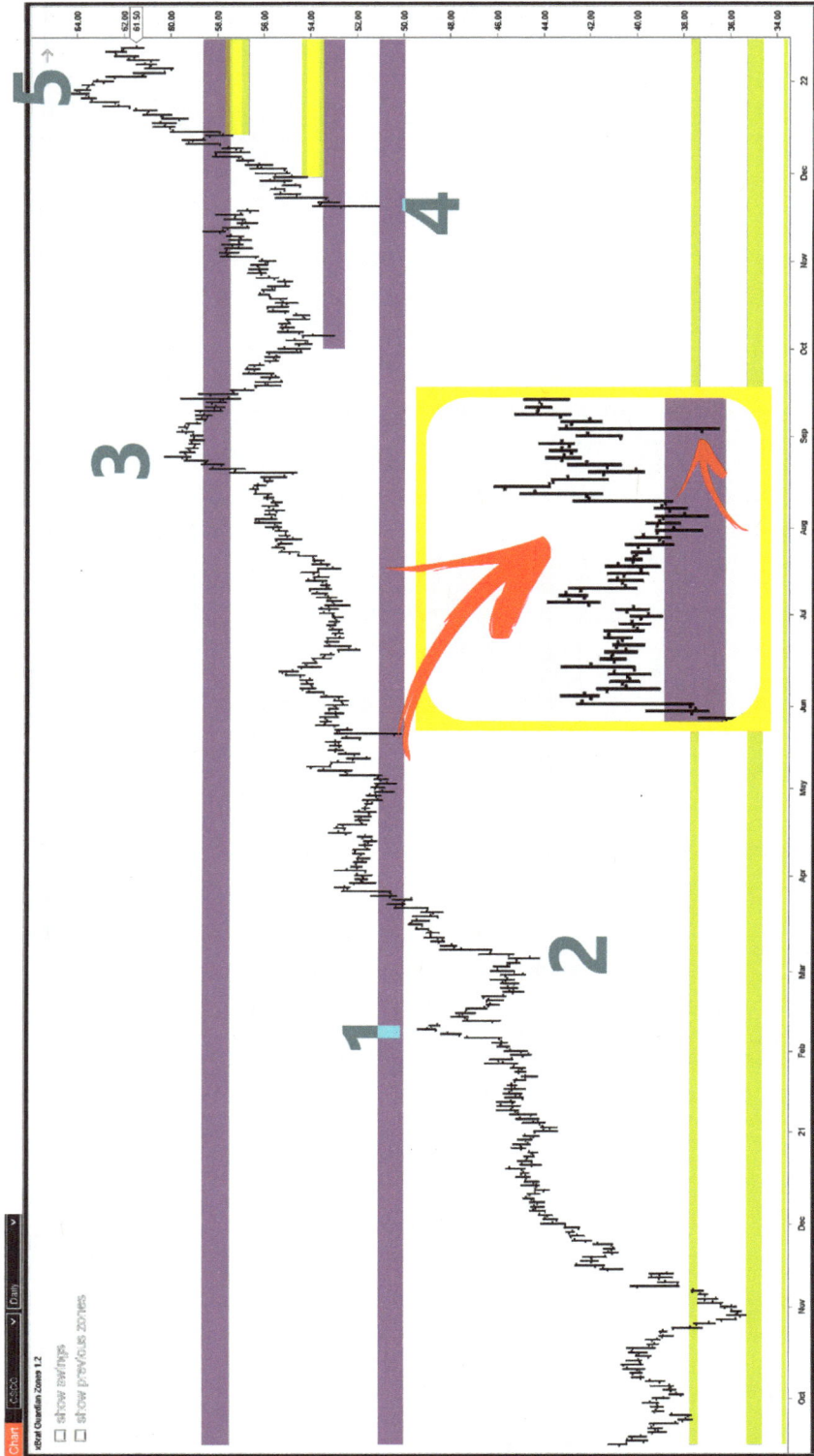

Chart 7.2 – Adding Support and Resistance to Help Identify Decision-Making During a Trend.

ELLIOTT WAVE THEORY

Before we continue to discuss the remainder of the move and where the next trading opportunity was, I want to introduce a simple version of the Elliott Wave Theory and the software that makes it easy to implement and use.

The herd mentality of traders (and the resulting reactions) forms patterns of movement/momentum within these cycles and data points. The Elliott Wave Theory is a useful tool that can label and represent this pattern in a meaningful way.

The Elliott Wave Theory is named after Ralph Nelson Elliott, who concluded that the movement of the stock market could be predicted by observing and identifying a repetitive pattern of waves. He also determined that these patterns hold true for both bear and bullish trends. It is basically a common-sense method of measuring the herd mentality of the markets.

Elliott Wave trading can be very complicated, with some traders and educators talking about 13 waves, inner waves, corrections, and some other convoluted technical nonsense! They then talk about ABC corrections and complex corrections — all trying to sound clever! This totally overcomplicates what is, at its core, a simple interpretation of trends.

If we keep it simple by concentrating on the hard Elliott Wave rules that cannot be broken and combine these with important observations using simple indicators, then we can create a simple and repeatable Elliott Wave trading strategy.

Wave 5 of an Elliott Wave sequence, by its nature, is the highest probability move in a trend since all the other hard rules and the majority of important observations have been

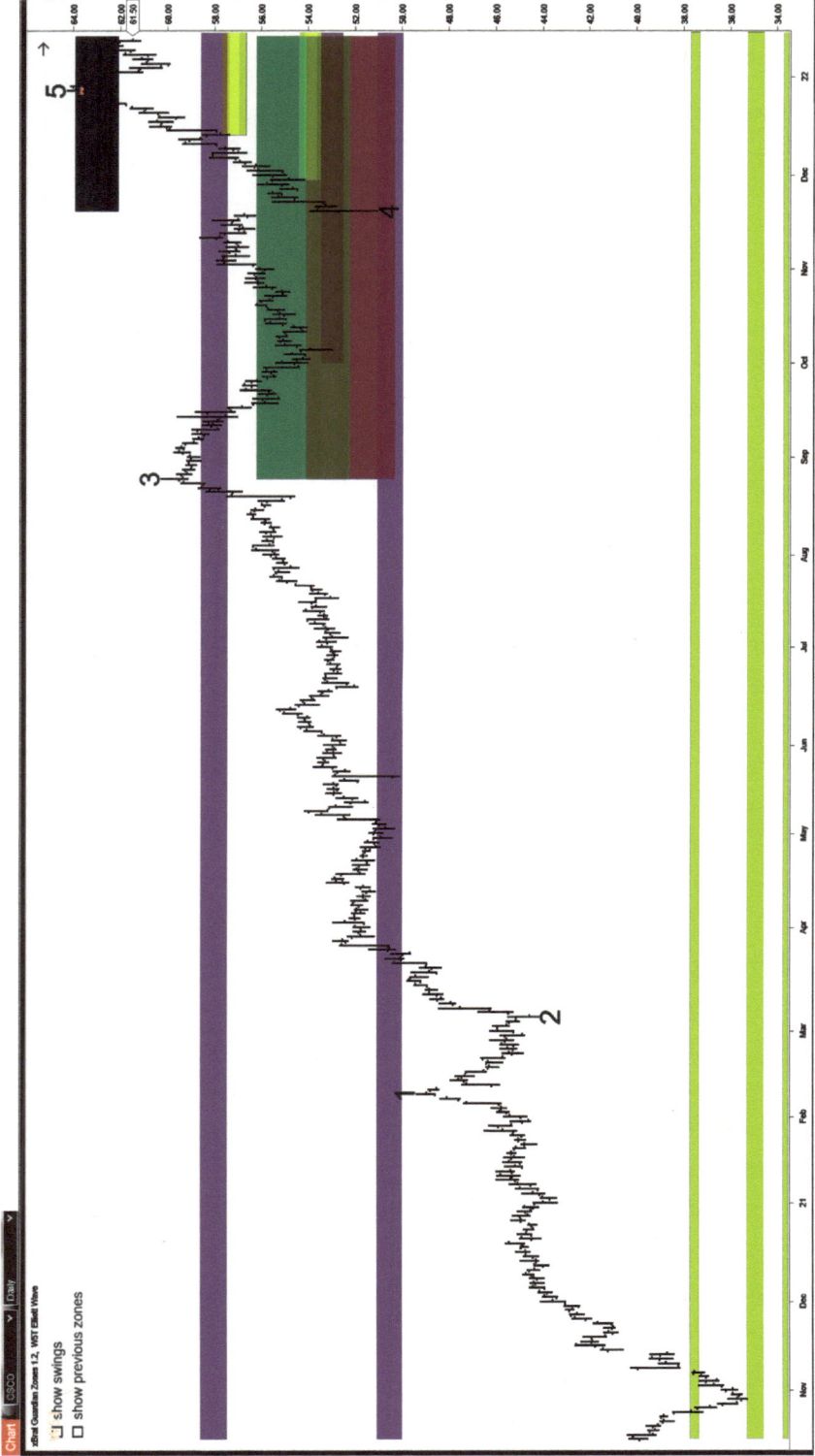

Chart 7.3 – Introducing Elliott Wave to the Same CSCO Chart, with Emphasis on Confluences on Wave 4.

met in the lead-up to a Wave 5 move. So, this is the "simple and repeatable Elliott Wave trading strategy" that we are looking for. Trading that moves on Chart 7.2 from point 4 to point 5.

By only concentrating on trading this highest probability move of an Elliott Wave sequence, we can block out all the other noise and concentrate on a simple set of rules!

Now, on Chart 7.3 for CSCO, I have removed my annotations and replaced them with the xBrat Elliott Wave trading indicator. The impulse moves, which we will now call waves, are labelled the same. The software now adds Fibonacci retracement pullback zones, where green is an 85 percent probability of hitting the automated Wave 5 target zone in blue. Amber is an 80 percent probability, and red is a 75 percent probability. We see that the Wave 4 pivot finds support at the confluence of the weekly support zone and

the red pullback zone and then starts to return to the bullish trend.

I have zoomed into the Wave 4 pivot on Chart 7.4 to make it easier to visualise and discuss one further confluence and the trigger for an aggressive entry long on CSCO. The candle that forms the Wave 4 pivot after the gap down from earnings rejected the lows at the confluence support mentioned above. But also note this happened

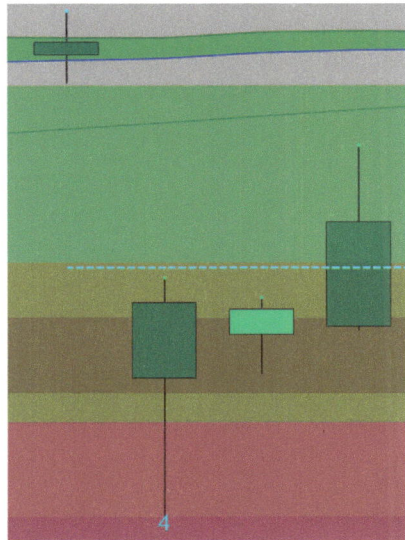

Chart 7.4 – Confluence and Entry Strategy for Wave 5 Trade.

with more volume than the previous day and with higher-than-average volume.

Using the xBrat Manager (a volume behaviour logic software), the cyan dot above the candle indicates higher than average volume, and the fact that the candle is coloured green means it's an accumulation candle (rather than a grey candle, which with this software, is an up candle but with less volume). When this perfect storm occurs, an aggressive entry long above the high of this day's candle (cyan-dashed line) would always be used to initially fill the gap and then trade Wave 5.

What about getting in the trend earlier? This is where a multiple-timeframe approach is needed with different trading strategies. The same CSCO chart is shown in Chart 7.5, but it's on a weekly timeframe. A bullish trend channel is on the chart now, with the upper trend line taken from the previous low in March 2020, after the pandemic pullback and a strong confluence of support at the 3rd target zone (red) for the bearish slingshot trade and the start of a **trend reversal**.

The xBrat SlingShot, first mentioned in the day trading chapter, has been used here to measure and trade the first pullback of this bullish trend after the lows in March 2020. Remember, for the daily charts, this was the Wave 2 pullback, and I mentioned that most traders would look to buy shares when it broke the Wave 1 pivot and through the weekly resistance zone around $50 (yellow on this weekly chart, as this is the colour of the native timeframe with the Guardian Zones Software). So now we have confluence using a different strategy on a different timeframe that is confirming that trade idea.

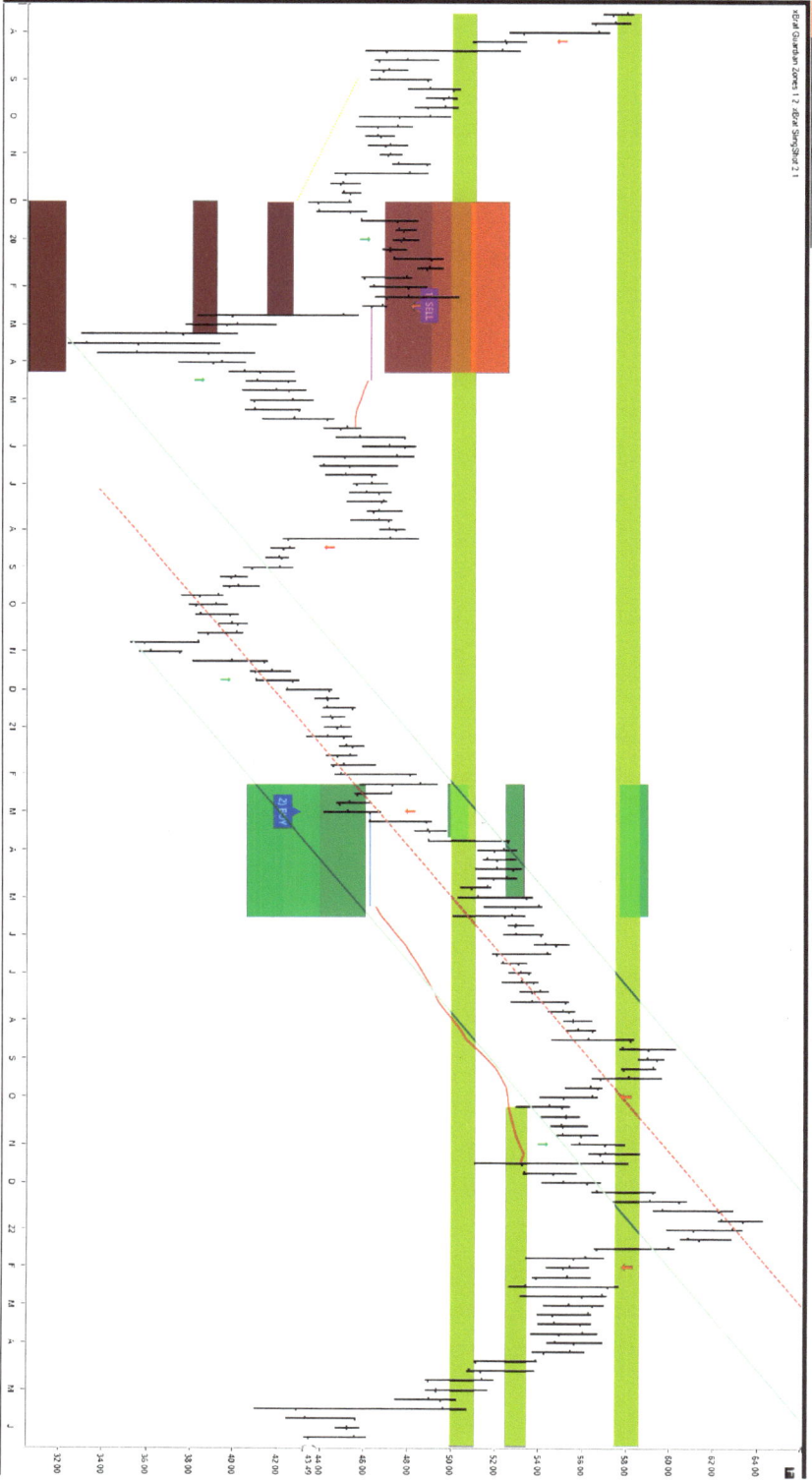

Chart 7.5 – Weekly Timeframe Chart of CSCO with Further Confluences.

TREND REVERSALS

When traders combine diverse indicators, they can create a more complete picture of market trend behaviour. The confluence of these indicators can provide a stronger signal that a trend reversal may be about to occur. For example, let's say a trader sees that a stock is approaching a key Fibonacci retracement or extension level and also approaching a strong support level. If they also note that an earnings report or a major news event is forthcoming, this could indicate that a trend reversal may be imminent.

In Chart 7.6, we see an example of the daily timeframe using the same CSCO stock, where the Wave 5 target zone (or Fibonacci extension resistance zone) is tested around the centre line of the channel that was drawn on the weekly timeframe. Also, this was the highest stock price that CSCO had achieved in a little over twenty years. With a confluence so strong, investors decided to take profits with enough volume to start a trend reversal that was again measured with the Elliott Wave.

After a move back up to test that infamous $50 support and resistance zone when earnings were released in late August 2022 (red arrow), we had another 1,2,3,4,5 move down. Then, a bounce off the Fibonacci extension Wave 5 target zone followed shortly after earnings in November 2022.

We see a bullish trend form with the Wave 5 target zone being hit around the $53 price. A correction down to test the strong daily support zone in yellow, just below the last pullback zone on the right of the chart, gives enough momentum to breach the $50 support and resistance zone, come back to test it as support, and then move past the recent Wave 5 pivot.

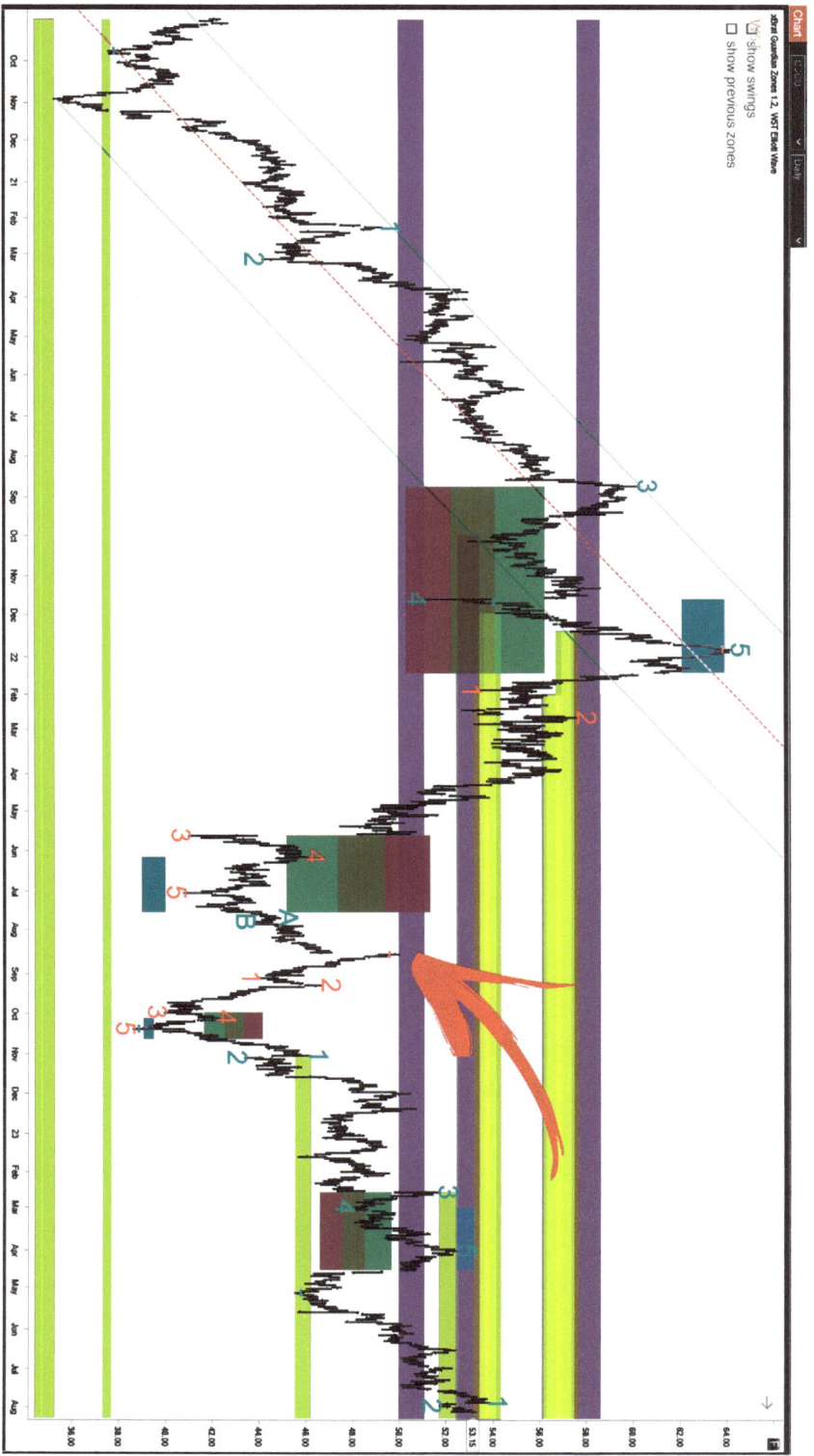

Chart 7.6 – Trend Reversals and More Measured Trends for CSCO with Elliott Wave.

The CSCO chart continues trending, but our review ends here, during the summer of 2023, when I finished writing this book.

Again, confluences of multiple elements are at play in many stocks that trend, including earnings, support and resistance, channels, and Elliott Wave Fibonacci extension to form the Wave 5 target zone!

CONCLUSION

Understanding trend behaviour is critical for successful trading and investing in financial markets. The simplified version of Elliott Wave provides a useful tool for measuring trends and identifying potential reversal points. Additionally, incorporating confluences with support and resistance zones enhances the accuracy of trend analysis.

By utilizing these techniques, traders and investors can make informed decisions based on a more complete picture of market trends. It is important to note, however, that while trend analysis can provide valuable insights, market conditions are constantly changing, and it is essential to continually evaluate and adapt strategies accordingly. By combining technical analysis with fundamental analysis and staying informed about global economic and geopolitical events, traders and investors can effectively navigate the complexities of financial markets and achieve their investment goals.

CHAPTER 8

Swing Trading and Confluences

SWING TRADING IS defined as the use of technical analysis to identify short- to medium-term opportunities in a trending security and, potentially, to profit from the price changes. It is an active trading strategy that requires traders to monitor market conditions, set trading plans, manage risk effectively, and, of course, look for confluences.

Swing trading is a popular approach in financial markets and typically involves holding a position for a short to medium period of time in order to capture potential gains from a price swing or market trend. Swing trading is not just limited to stocks. Traders also look to swing trade forex and futures, and recently, even cryptocurrency has become an option. Whereas investing, another form of swing trading, is predominantly for buying and holding stocks longer term, which could be a year or, in my case, ten years or more.

In this chapter, I want to cover shorter-term swings where traders typically hold a position for a few days but very rarely carry it over a weekend. With this idea, I'll look at swing trading futures, though forex works pretty much the same. Medium-term swing trading in stocks will also be looked at, along with longer-term investing strategies for stocks. We'll examine confluences between technical analysis, technical indicator strategies, options activity, and fundamental data to highlight specific strong confluences that traders and investors should look for and not ignore.

SHORT-TERM SWING TRADING

Short-term swing trading aims to take advantage of short-term changes in a stock's overall price trajectory. To illustrate this, I have chosen the US 10-year bond futures contract ($ZN) as an example of a great, steady instrument for short-term swing trading on a 30-minute timeframe.

The value of the 10-year US bond futures is derived from the underlying U.S. Treasury bond, which is a debt instrument issued by the US government to raise funds for its operations. These bonds are considered to be low-risk investments, as they are backed by the full faith and credit of the US government. Additionally, the interest rate paid on these bonds is closely watched by investors because it serves as a benchmark for other interest rates in the market.

Traders use 10-year US bond futures to hedge their exposure to interest rate risk and to gain exposure to the broader bond market. If traders believe that interest rates are going to rise, they may go short on the futures contracts, anticipating that the price of the underlying bond will decline. On the other hand, if they think that interest rates will fall, they may go long on futures contracts, hoping bond prices will increase.

The economic data points for this larger confluence are not daily. They usually occur only once a month. Therefore, trends are easier to identify and tend to reverse/start with inflation or interest data from either the United States or, indeed, Europe. We can't forget those correlations!

The correlation between the 10-year US bond futures and the US dollar stems from their close relationship to US government debt. When the market believes that the US government's creditworthiness is strong and that U.S. Treasury bonds are a safe investment, demand for these bonds increases, pushing up their price and lowering their yield. This, in turn, tends to strengthen the US dollar as investors flock to the safety and stability of the US economy.

Conversely, when the market perceives that the US government's creditworthiness is weak, demand for U.S. Treasury bonds falls, causing their price to drop and their yield to rise. In such a scenario, investors may prefer to hold other currencies or assets that they perceive to be less risky, causing the US dollar to weaken.

The movements of the 10-year US bond futures and the S&P 500 futures are closely watched by investors and traders alike. The two instruments are widely considered reliable measures of risk and yield, with one reflecting the fixed-income market and the other showing the performance of the stock market. The direction of longer-term bond trends is also influenced by wider, more macro confluences.

Firstly, economic growth plays a critical role in affecting bond trends. When the economy is experiencing a period of robust growth, there is a greater demand for credit as businesses seek to finance projects to capitalize on the growth momentum. Consequently, there is an upswing in the demand for bonds to fund these credit endeavours, which drives up bond prices and lowers yields. In contrast, a sluggish economy with weak growth prospects tends to cause a decline in the demand for credit, leading to lower bond prices and higher yields.

Secondly, inflation is another significant macro factor that influences long-term bond trends. Inflationary pressures emanate from a range of sources, including rising commodity prices, expanding fiscal policies, or wage hikes. Inflation erodes the value of fixed-rate bonds, and, as a result, investors demand a higher yield to offset the losses incurred due to inflation. Therefore, inflationary pressures usually drive up yields, which lowers bond prices. In contrast, deflationary pressures typically result in lower yields, which translates to higher bond prices.

CORRELATIONS

Historical data shows that correlations between the two futures have existed for years, although the extent and direction of these correlations have varied depending on market conditions and other factors. Exploring some examples of these correlations can give us insight into how they may impact investors and traders.

One notable period of correlation occurred during the 2007–2008 financial crisis. In the months leading up to the crisis, investors fled the stock market in droves, seeking the relative safety of Treasury bonds. As a result, bond yields fell sharply, and the price of Treasury futures rose. At the same time, the S&P 500 was in freefall, experiencing the worst declines since the Great Depression.

During this period, the negative correlation between the two instruments was particularly strong. As the S&P 500 continued to decline, the price of Treasury futures continued to rise, reflecting growing concerns about the state of the economy. This trend persisted until early 2009, when the Federal Reserve cut interest rates to encourage borrowing and spending, and the stock market began to stabilize.

A more recent example of correlation occurred in early 2020 when the COVID-19 pandemic rattled global markets. As the pandemic spread across the world, investors once again flocked to safe-haven assets like U.S. Treasury bonds, leading to a sharp rise in bond prices and a drop in bond yields. Meanwhile, the S&P 500 experienced one of its worst quarters ever, shedding more than 30 percent of its value between February and March 2020.

ONE WEEK IN THE LIFE OF $ZN FUTURES

Since swing trading takes place over a few days, I want to follow the path of a US 10-year bond swing trade over the course of one week. Specifically, it will be the week that commenced 31 July 2023 — the summer during which I was writing this book. I chose this week because a great catalyst occurred on Monday of that week when European inflation data was released around one hour after the London open, which you can see on Chart 8.1. While the chart looks quite busy, I will, as usual, start from the left and talk through each section, all confluences, and every trading decision, and again, you can view digital versions of the charts at PaulBratby.com/Book-Club.

I'm not going to share higher timeframes, but just know that the main trend on the daily timeframe since April 2023 has been down, and then later in the weekly chart, since COVID-19, the trend has been bearish. So short/bearish signals are preferred with these confluences in mind. The grey trend channel is taken from the 60-minute timeframe for this current move down.

The open Sunday and overnight has the price continuing down until touching the lower bound around the same time as the London open. The confluence of the London/European stock market opens and the non-linear support was enough for the price of $ZN to go up, labelling Wave 3 of this current bearish trend on the 30-minute timeframe. The Wave 4 pullback went through the US morning and found resistance at the confluence of the 30- and 60-minute resistance zones and the red pullback zone on the Elliott Wave software — too much for the price to push through, especially as overall, the BONDS are on a longer-term bearish trend.

Here is the first swing trading opportunity on $ZN for this week. The Wave 4 was quite orderly in that the trend channel was nice and tight. Add this to the confluences just mentioned, and most traders would look for an aggressive short entry as the price breaks down out of the Wave 4 trend channel. I personally prefer to wait for the breakout candle to close and place the order below the low, represented in this chart by the red arrow and red hashed line. We then see an xBratAlgo 5* SELL signal form. Remember, a confluence of eleven out of twelve points of control is needed for this signal.

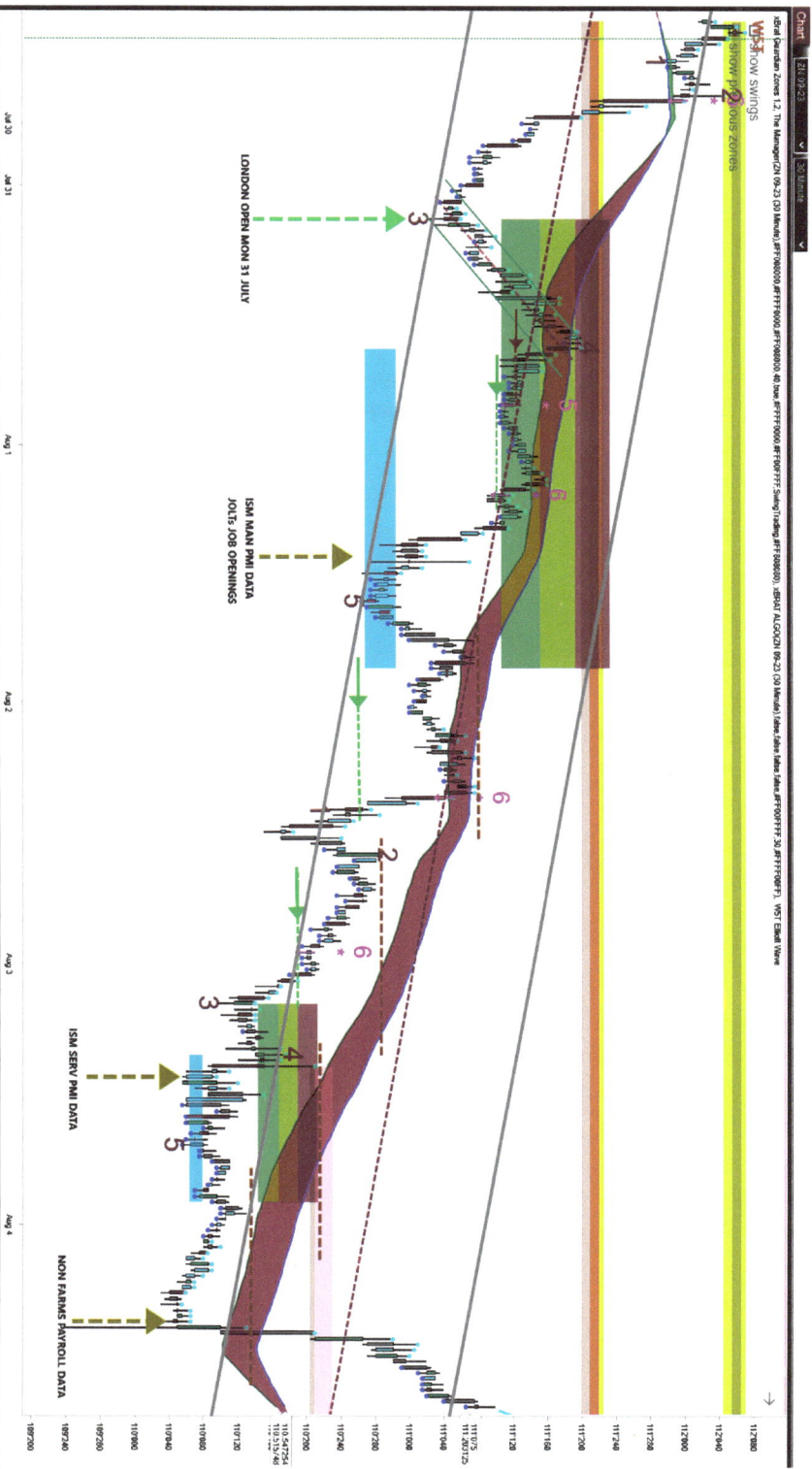

Chart 8.1 – Short-Term Swing Trading with Futures.

So, now we have all the previous confluences of support and resistance, pullback zones, and Elliott Wave short signal Wave 5. But we have a short signal from a completely different strategy (too strong to miss if we didn't take the aggressive entry!) with an entry short at the green arrow and hashed lines just under the aggressive entry of the red arrow. There was a further xBratAlgo 6* SELL later as the short trade was taken in on Tuesday (1 August 2023), an hour after the London/European open, giving more confidence.

This initial move on 1 August 2023 found initial support at the confluence of the Wave 5 target zone and the lower bound of the 60-minute trend channel. At this same time, we had ISM Manufacturing PMI data and JOLTS job openings data, both of which are catalysts for the US dollar and, therefore, based on correlations for US bonds. From this point, traders can take two paths.

THE FIRST PATH

The first and sensible path for traders with less experience in confluence trading is to identify the strong confluence of the Wave 5 target zone being hit and, at the same time, test the lower bound of the 60-minute trend channel. Making the decision to take the profit before the data would close this first swing trade for the week on $ZN and have around $540 profit for each contract traded. I usually start the week with three contracts.

Then, look for further short opportunities during the week. During this week, there were two more 6* SELL signals. The very next one was strong, as the catalyst was the

US gold pit open on 2 August. This trade would have stayed on for the remainder of the week until just before the Nonfarm Payroll Data on Friday. The Nonfarm Payroll data set is one of the biggest data points on the calendar, and all swing trading positions should be closed before this! I will cover the reasons why positions should be closed as I discuss the second path since the logic is the same. The Second 6* SELL signal came after the Bank of England interest rate decision at 7 a.m. UK time on the third of August. This is a great example of a further catalyst to add to the confluences, sending the price of $ZN down. The flow downward just got faster as another tributary joined!

THE SECOND PATH

The second path is the one I take and is geared towards traders with more confluence trading experience who know how to use xBrat Manager. For me, if I can get in a short-term swing trade on a Monday or Tuesday, my aim is to

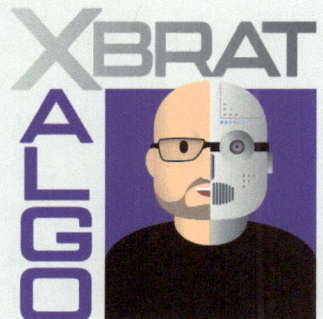

add more contracts to the trade as the week goes on. I add more contracts when (and ONLY when) I get further signals and confluences, usually after pullbacks against the main trend of the week. This takes practice and the ability to understand all the confluences I discuss in this book, which is helped in a large part by software.

I've mentioned the xBrat Manager and want to expand a little now on the volume and price action behaviour it shows by providing a real example. Let's start with the move up from the Wave 5 target zone and the confluence of the lower bound of the 60-minute trend channel. This move up has blue dots below the candles, which means the bullish move had lower-than-average volume. The last four candles before the price found resistance at the centre line of the 60-minute trend channel were grey. So, each candle was an up candle but had less volume compared to the preceding candle. This behaviour shows that the move is running out of momentum or, as I like to say, "running out of juice."

As far as managing those first three contract shorts is concerned, I don't panic about the lack of momentum because the xBrat Manager ribbon remains red (ribbon on swing trading setting), and the centre line resistance is holding. These strong confluences allow me not to worry and to expect a resumption of the bearish trend. Then, the price moves back down but with lower-than-average volume. This pivot formed at the centre line of the 60-minute trend channel is a focal point. At this point, to reduce risk, I place a trailing stop just after the entry price to make it a "risk-free" trade.

We then get another test of this pivot, which holds and forms a double top chart pattern around the US gold pit open on 2 August. The first action to be taken here is to adjust the trailing stop one tick above the pivots, forming this double top as the price breaking the low pivot of this chart pattern as the next xBratAlgo 6* SELL signal is formed. Another set of strong confluences then triggers a further move down.

The next action is to add one contract to this trade as the price action breaks through the low of the previous Wave 5 target zone (green arrow and hashed line). A more aggressive entry would be one tick below the low of the 6* SELL signal candle. I personally prefer price to clear danger. We get a Wave 2 pullback then and a perfect place to lock in profit by adjusting the trailing stop (orange hashed line).

The next option is to add another contract to this short trade on the next xBratAlgo 6* SELL signal or the break of the low pivot before the Wave 2. Then, the trend has a pullback on 3 August 2023 to form a Wave 4 on our Elliott Wave software, just before the ISM Services PMI data is released. Trading this Wave 5 is not advisable so close to data. But this provides us with an opportunity to adjust the trailing stop one tick above the Wave 4 high pivot price. It's important to note the confluences between the wave being formed and the higher-than-average volume rejection of the highs of the Wave 4, as depicted with the help of the xBrat Manager in Chart 8.1, which depicts a good 50 percent retracement on that 30-minute candle.

At this point, notice how the range period forms around this latest Wave 5 Fibonacci extension zone. Going into Friday, 4 August, the price tests the lower bound of the 60-minute trend channel from below and rejects the move up. This is the last trailing stop adjustment and is meant to lock in more profit before the biggest data release of the week, the Nonfarm Payroll, at 08:30 a.m. EST. With so much profit locked in on the five contracts, I generally then let the data come out and see if the reaction takes us further down. In this case, it didn't. About an hour after the data was released, the trailing stop was taken out, and around $3,000 profit was earned.

Obviously, flattening the position before data would have made approximately another $1,000 profit, but hindsight isn't a trading strategy. For me, it's better to have a decent profit locked in and then look for those runners after data that can boost your profits considerably. In cases where I have "fresh air" and good profits locked in with my trailing stop, I take this strategic course of action and have seen around sixty percent of reactions to data move in the direction of my trade and the trend. In this case, this did not happen, and it was a catalyst for short-term reversal that was tradeable the following week.

MEDIUM-TERM SWING TRADING – STOCKS

Medium-term swing trading of stocks refers to a trading strategy that involves buying and holding stocks for a period of time ranging from a few weeks to several months, with the aim of profiting from the price fluctuations in the market. This strategy requires an understanding of confluences with technical and fundamental analysis, as well as the ability to identify stocks that have the potential to fluctuate significantly in the short term.

Apple Inc. ($AAPL) is generally too big for short-term swing trades, but it still has room for growth, which makes it a better medium-term swing trade. AAPL stock has a high trading volume, making it easier to enter and exit positions quickly as market trends shift. The stock has a daily average trading volume of over 60 million shares, indicating a high level of liquidity, which is essential for swing trading. Moreover, AAPL's frequent price fluctuations offer ample opportunities for traders to capitalize on short-term price movements.

I also want to touch on Apple's confluence with the S&P 500. As mentioned earlier in the book, Apple stock is a large component of the S&P 500, which means its intercorrelations, major support and resistance zones, and overall behavioural confluences are important to consider.

In addition to these technical factors, the overall market sentiment surrounding Apple is also worth keeping in mind. The company's recent earnings reports, February and May 2023, have been strong, exhibiting strong growth in both its services and wearables divisions. At the same time, concerns about the iPhone's long-term growth prospects have led some investors to question whether the company can maintain its current momentum.

CONFLUENCES AND MEDIUM-TERM SWING TRADING

Before delving into swing trading Apple, I want to introduce two new confluence factors that are particularly relevant for medium-term swing trading and investing — unusual options activity and insider trading. Like other factors discussed, understanding these can enhance and confirm decisions to take positions, exit positions, or, indeed, not get into a position in the first place.

Unusual Options Activity

Tracking unusual options activity is a popular strategy institutional traders use to hedge their positions. This activity refers to when a stock's option contracts are trading at a higher-than-normal rate. The unusual activity can be the result of a few large trades by institutional traders or reflect widespread interest in a stock. It is also important to keep in mind the timing of options expiration and the chosen strike price. These critical factors can help traders understand unusual options activity.

Typically, option contracts have fixed expiration dates, which means the holder of the option has the right to execute a trade at a particular strike price until that expiration date. Traders may choose either a short- or long-term expiration date based on their trading strategy. A common short-term strategy involves choosing an expiration date that coincides with a stock's earnings date, which often causes significant short-term price movements.

Institutional traders frequently use options contracts to hedge their positions, buying or selling options contracts to mitigate risk or potential losses. However, unusual options activity may suggest that institutional traders are either hedging or betting against a particular stock's price movement. For instance, if an institutional trader sees high trading volume inputs (options contracts giving the holder the right but not the obligation to sell the underlying asset at a predetermined price), they may interpret this as an indication of bearish sentiment towards the stock.

Additionally, unusual options activity may occur before a company's earnings release, indicating that institutional traders are taking positions ahead of pending earnings announcements. For example, unusually high trading activity in call options (options contracts giving the holder the right but not the obligation to buy the underlying asset at a predetermined price) before an earnings announcement implies that institutional traders may be positioning themselves for a potential positive earnings surprise.

Insider Activity

Insider activity refers to trading activity conducted by shareholders who have access to crucial information that can impact the financial performance of the company they are invested in. The US Securities and Exchange Commission (SEC) requires such insider activity to be reported to help safeguard against illegal insider trading practices.

When insiders trade using nonpublic information, it can result in unfair gains, thereby threatening the integrity of the financial markets. Consequently, the SEC requires all insiders, including executives, directors, and large shareholders, to report their trading activity to the public. Such reporting helps investors understand the overall activity of insiders within a company. In fact, the SEC requires insiders to report any transaction involving company stock, including purchases, sales, and options exercise, within two business days of the trade, and this information is available to the public via various mediums, including company filings, external websites, and financial reports.

Having access to this data can help investors make more informed investment decisions, particularly leading up to a company's earnings release. Insider activity can offer valuable insights regarding the confidence insiders have in their company's prospects. For instance, if insiders purchase shares of their company just before its earnings release, it may indicate that they expect positive earnings results. On the other hand, if insiders sell shares ahead of an earnings release, it may indicate negative performance expectations.

Investors can use insider activity data to identify trends and patterns over time. Consistent insider buying activity can signal bullish sentiment, indicating a positive long-term outlook for the company. Conversely, consistent insider selling activity can signal bearish sentiment, indicating a negative long-term outlook for the company.

APPLE STOCK – $AAPL

Now, let's get back to swing trading and Apple ($AAPL). Chart 8.2 illustrates $AAPL on the daily timeframe for 2023. As usual, we will work from the left side of the chart and discuss trend analysis and confluences. But first, the inset chart with a yellow border is the S&P 500 on the daily timeframe and shows a strong weekly resistance zone in magenta at the end of July 2023. At the same time, $AAPL is struggling to make a further Wave 3 high. A very strong confluence of resistance that is happening just before an $AAPL earnings report cannot be ignored.

At the beginning of 2023, we can also see a strong start to a bullish trend. Then, the first earnings in February (first green down arrow, annotated "Earnings") came as the price was reaching a confluence of daily resistance zones. Consequently, a profit taking pullback occurred, giving us a Wave 1 pivot, marked on the chart.

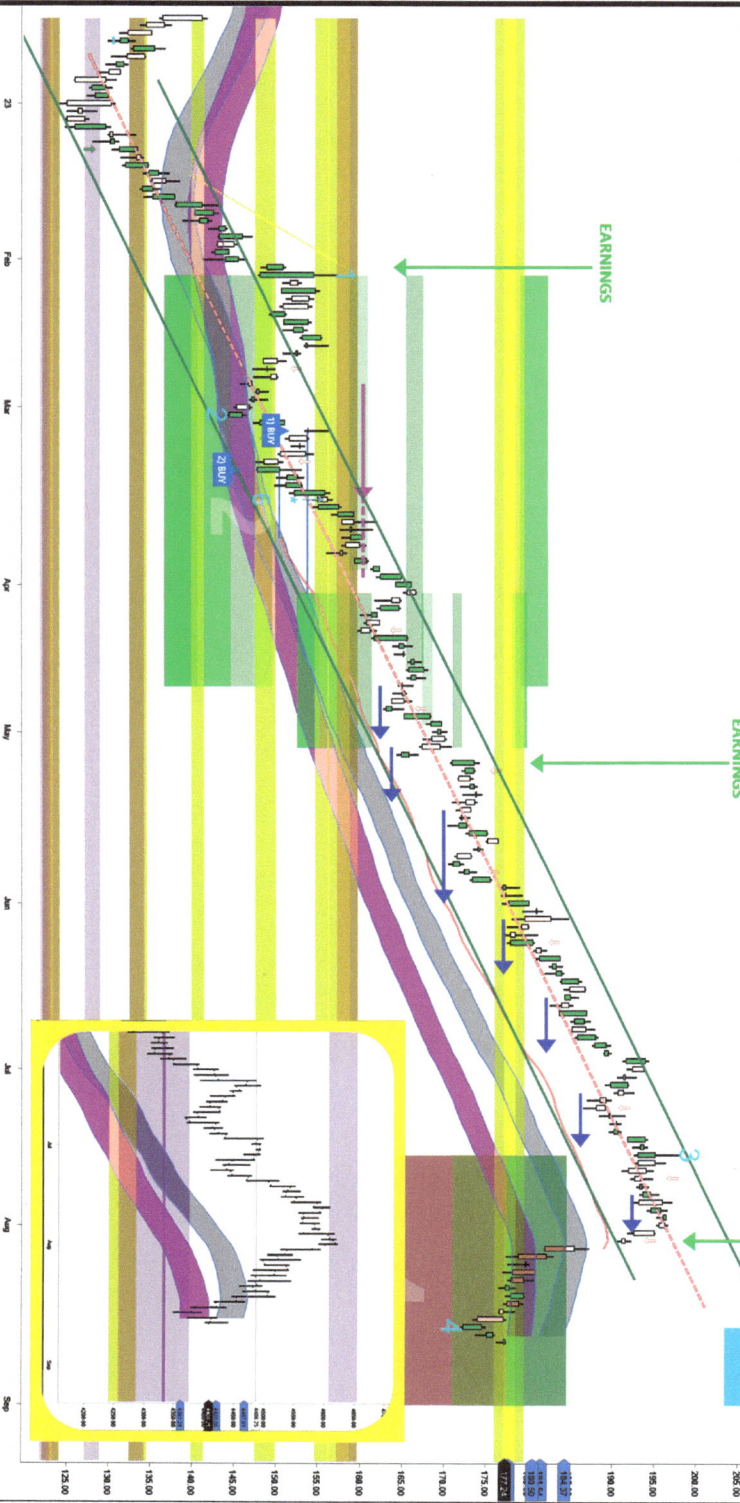

Chart 8.2 – Apple Inc. Daily Chart: Swing Trading Strategy with Confluences.

The Wave 2 pullback found support at the convergence of the 55 and 89 EMA Clouds and the first pullback zone of the xBrat SlingShot. Then, we have Type 1 and Type 2 buy signals from the slingshot, followed by an xBratAlgo 6* BUY signal — a massive confluence of technical analysis and signals from two completely different trading strategies. Be cautious here since all were signals into the previous resistance found by the Wave 1 pivot. Entry for the long swing trade on $AAPL would be above this resistance zone where the magenta arrow and hashed line are on the chart.

After entry, the price initially rises to test the second target of the slingshot, and then a slight pullback occurs to test the previous resistance zone, which now holds as support. We then see another slingshot pullback zone form, and the price finds support and returns to the bullish move. At this point, we have enough pivots to draw in a bullish trend channel, as seen on Chart 8.2.

The price then continues to rise within this tight, bullish channel, even though the next earnings announcement isn't until May. In fact, you can see that every time the price goes below the centre line of the channel on a pullback, we form higher lows, indicated by the blue arrows within the channel on the chart. This is a very strong bullish trend, and swing traders should stay in this trade until the pattern is broken.

On 8 July 2023, there was insider activity. A major shareholder sold 15,419 shares at a value of $178.56 and earned $2,753,216.64 whilst still holding onto 136,445 shares after the transaction. A nice, sizeable profit before earnings from someone with financial knowledge of the company! Image 8.3 shows the SEC Form 4 that insiders need to file when buying or selling company stock. This sale was not unusual for this particular shareholder, as past instances of selling before earnings have occurred. However, traders need to be aware of this data as more confluences occur. It just solidifies trading decisions.

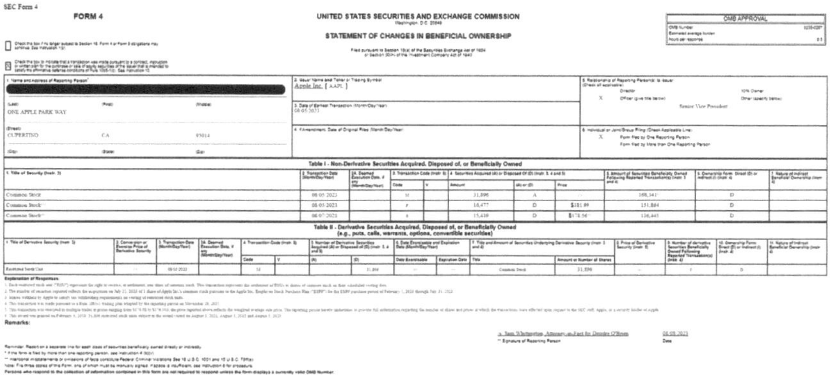

Image 8.3 – SEC Form 4 - Insider Buying or Selling Activity.

On 20 July 2023, at 15:15:22 EST, an unusually large $874.38K block of put contracts in Apple ($AAPL) was bought with a strike price of $195.00 per share, expiring on 11 August 2023. The volume of the purchased contracts was significant, indicating that the buyer could be a large institution or a high-net-worth individual. This purchase shows that the buyer either has significant concerns about Apple's future performance or was hedging their long position against a profit by taking pullback after earnings since the next earnings report was due in early August. Confluences like this from data outside of technical analysis and leading up to earnings cannot be ignored.

But back to our technical analysis, the bullish pattern of higher lows on pivots after shallow pullbacks is broken when a Wave 3 is formed on $AAPL. At the same time, the S&P 500 is finding strong resistance in the weekly timeframe, and it's only a couple of days until the $AAPL earnings report.

This overwhelming confluence of factors is a sign for swing traders — take profit before earnings. Remember, swing trading is not a long-term hold but rather a shorter-term commitment that involves riding a trend until the stars align and indicate a trend failure.

Confluence trading really helps simplify and maximise these decisions. In this case, the swing trade long on $AAPL was a little over four months. Swing trading requires stop losses, and in this case, the stop would need to be on the low pivot after the 2 pivot and before the 6* BUY signal. This gives a risk-to-reward ratio of 1:2 for this trade. Simply put, that's a 200 percent gain on initial risk!

Next, a swing trader monitors the Wave 4 profit taking pullback using the Elliott Wave software and looks for confluences and signals to indicate another swing trade on $AAPL in 2023. If none are showing, then there are NO swing trading opportunities! I will use $AAPL again when I discuss longer-term investing in stocks and when investors look to add to their positions on pullbacks with the aid of software and confluences.

TAKEAWAYS

Effective swing trading and investing in stocks combine unusual options activity and insider activity with standard technical analysis techniques as well as technical strategy signals. This generates a great deal of data and information for traders to gather and analyse!

This is why it became my mission to create a tool that could effectively and quickly aggregate this data so I could identify stocks with a multitude of fundamental, behavioural, and technical confluences. The end result? It's the xBrat Stocks Predator, and it hunts down stocks with stars aligned or, as we say in England, "ducks in a row."

STOCKS INVESTING – LONGER TERM

Again, I am going to use $AAPL as my trading example, but this time, over a seven-year period that ranges from July 2016 to July 2023, as shown in Chart 8.4. The seven-year example tells the story of simple stock investments with confluences involving pullbacks, earnings, unusual options activity, support and resistance, and insider activity. The pullbacks were measured, and signals were taken using the xBrat SlingShot, primarily with an Elliott Wave entry. In 2020, after the COVID-19 pandemic pullback, it found support at the 89 EMA cloud

Scan me!

Introducing the
xBrat Stocks Predator

The **xBrat Stocks Predator** is a stand alone dashboard utilising lots of the xBrat Software as well as exclusive fundamental scans and technical scans. Please scan the QR code for more information.

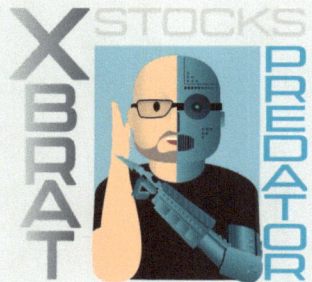

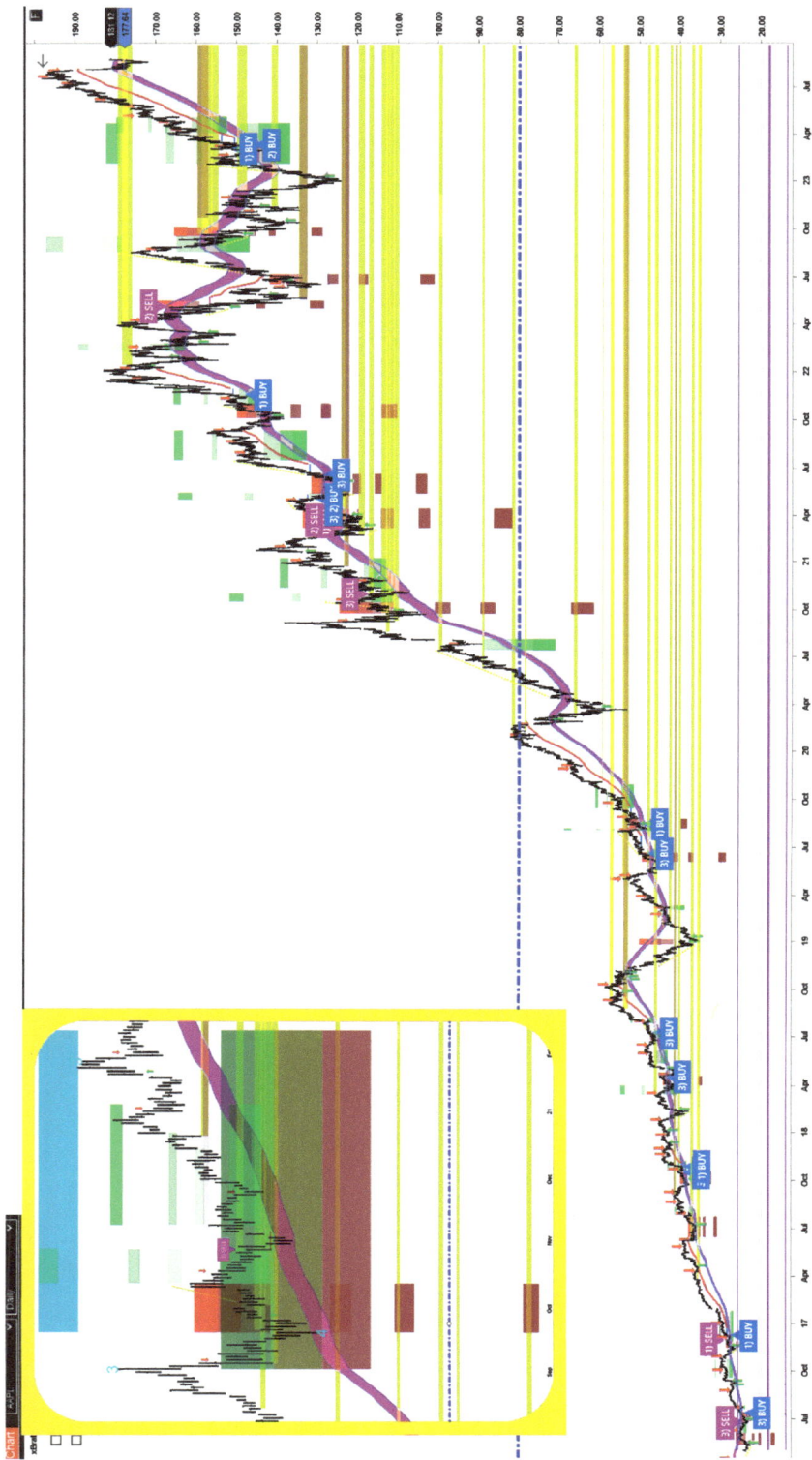

Chart 8.4 – Apple Inc. Over 7 Years on the Daily Timeframe, Longer-Term Investing Strategies with Confluences.

and the amber zone in the Elliott Wave probability pullback zones (inset on the chart). I won't go over old ground, but in each case, there were more than three confluences, as described earlier in this chapter. The rules for confluences do not change from short- and medium-term swing trading to longer-term investing. The only difference is that investors hold their positions and add to them on pullbacks with confluences present.

For this example, I chose a $1,000 investment in Apple Inc. shares at each signal with twelve entries in total during the seven-year period, with a total amount invested of $12,000. A total of 222 shares were purchased over this time period, and as of writing this book in the summer of 2023, the portfolio of $AAPL shares has an average holding price of approximately $80 and a current value of $40,208. That's a 335 percent return in seven years on just one stock. Those returns are impressive.

TAKEAWAYS

A final thought: long-term investors should not shy away from swing trading a stock in which they also have a long-term investment. Experienced traders and investors often apportion wealth into pots that can be used for swing trading, investing, and, in some cases (like mine), day trading as well. After all, with leveraged products like options, contracts for difference (CFDs), and futures, there are opportunities to make profits to feed the investing pot with more capital.

I discuss futures trading in chapter 6 and won't discuss options trading in this book. I simply don't use options as

I believe they are a convoluted system that is not needed when CFDs are basically like futures and very simple to use. CFDs have no shorting rules or borrowing stock. While they are not available in the United States, they are easily found in the rest of the world. Take away from that what you will!

SHORTING TO FEED THE INVESTING POT

In this section, I present an example and describe exactly how I traded it. But, before getting into those details, I briefly want to discuss the strength and resilience of the US stock market. The US stock market has exhibited impressive strength and resiliency, particularly in recent years. Tech stocks have been the driving force of this performance, having proven resilient in the aftermath of the previous dot-com bubble burst. In fact, tech stocks have emerged as some of the largest and most influential constituents of the S&P 500. Let's face it: we all rely on lots of tech in our everyday lives, which makes it a logical investment.

Recent global events have tested the mettle of the US stock market, but it has continually bounced back in a positive direction. Take, for example, the pandemic-induced market downturn in 2020. Despite widespread economic disruption and uncertainty, the market quickly regained its footing and surged to new heights, powered in large part by the continued strength of tech stocks. I learned much more from this recovery in terms of short-term swing trading. I started swing trading down and then used the profits to purchase more shares in the same stock.

I have used this type of strategy since 2013. But since 2018, this approach has proven particularly successful in the context of US tech stocks, which have consistently shown their ability to rebound from market shocks and emerge stronger than ever. With their propensity for innovation and constant adaptation, US tech stocks are well-positioned to weather any market fluctuations and remain a key driver of economic growth.

Similarly, the recent Russian invasion of Ukraine in 2022 caused a sharp dip in markets around the world. However, US markets demonstrated a remarkable ability to weather the crisis, posting gains within days of the initial shock and continuing to experience sustained growth in the months since. My thinking is that if we can recover from a catastrophic pandemic that previously was only ever in the movies, then the markets can recover from just about anything. During these times, I focused all my trades on the shorts I could take with the ultimate goal of using the profits to purchase physical shares in the same stock.

These examples serve as compelling evidence of the strength and resiliency of the US stock market, particularly when it comes to tech stocks. Despite past and present challenges, investors can trust in the potential for continued growth and success in this dynamic and influential segment of the market. Obviously, I don't just press the short button. I need confluences to stack up to give me the confidence to take the shorts.

In this example, I look at swing trading short on Microsoft stock ($MSFT) following large catalysts for pullbacks. Chart 8.5 shows the weekly timeframe on $MSFT, the pandemic pullback between Waves 1 and 2, and the Russian invasion of

Ukraine between Waves 3 and 4. Notice how the Elliot Wave 4 pullback did, in fact, find support in the pullback zones, and Microsoft recovered from this large geopolitical catalyst.

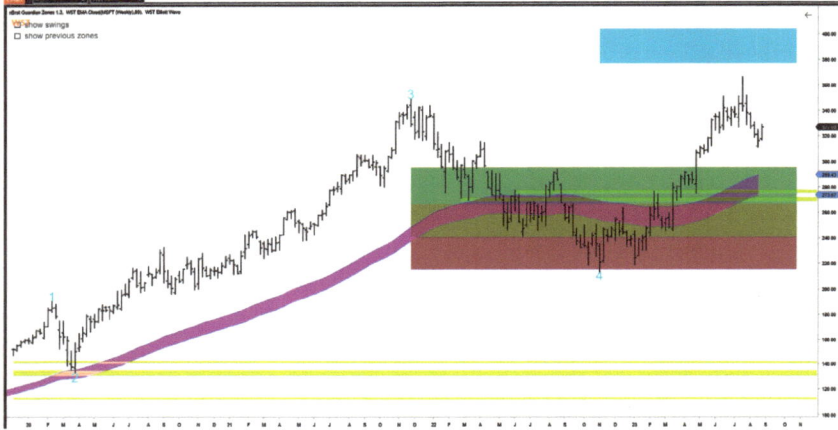

Chart 8.5 – Shorting Microsoft ($MSFT): Confluence Catalysts.

SHORTING $MSFT DURING COVID-19 PULLBACK

At the end of January 2020, Microsoft made an earnings announcement that was decent enough, but this was trumped by the gathering momentum of COVID-19. The beginnings of the pandemic initially stalled the strong bullish trend that $MSFT was enjoying. Then, as the world started to panic in the grip of this new, unfathomable phenomenon, all stock prices started to come down as investors were taking off risk.

Chart 8.6 shows how Microsoft was shorted during COVID-19. Just before the end of February 2020, an xBrat Algo 5* SELL signal was printed on the daily timeframe for

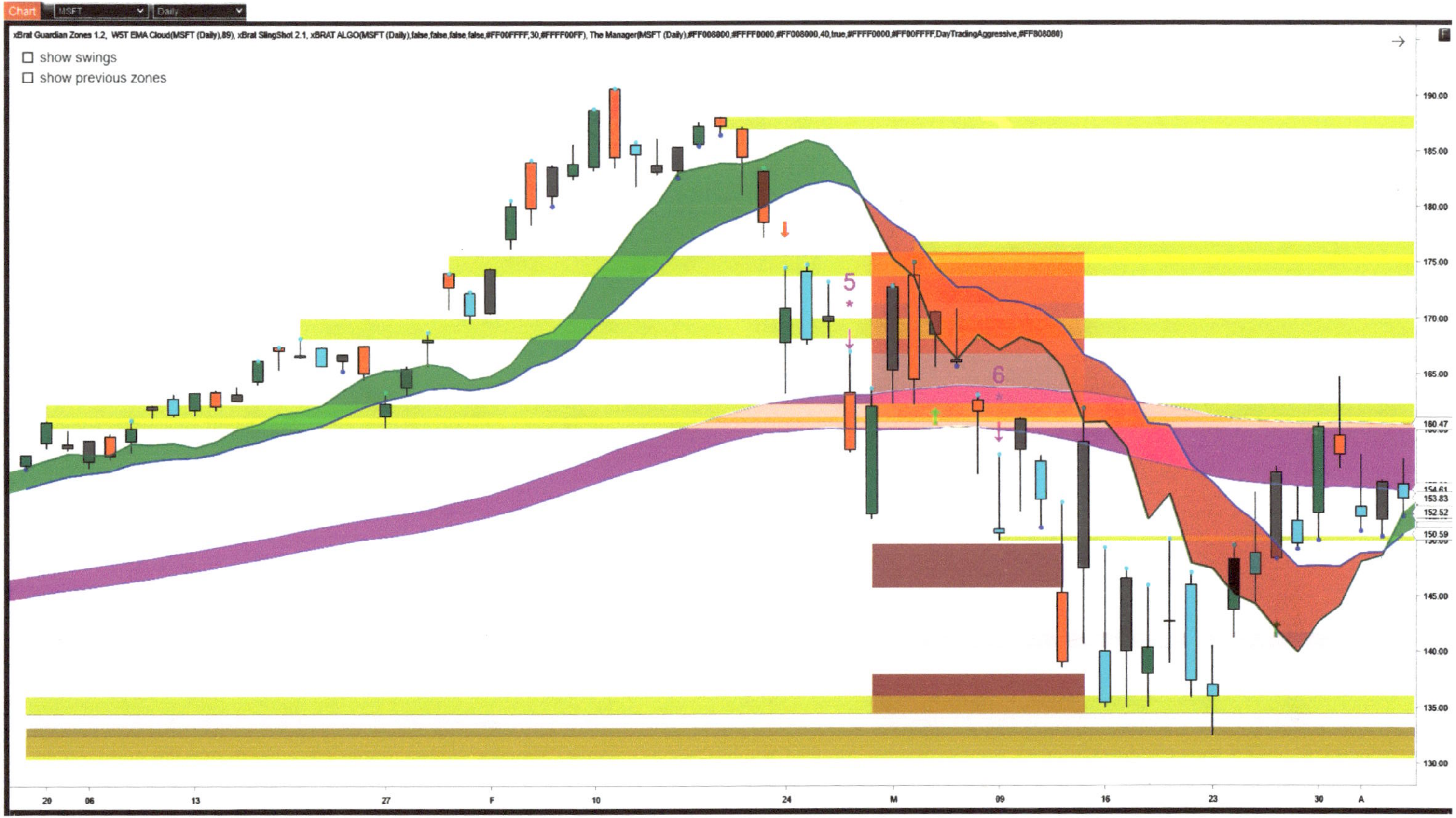

Chart 8.6 – Shorting $MSFT During COVID-19.

$MSFT after breaking a daily support zone. A confluence of COVID-19 reactions, a technical signal to sell, and breaking support were enough for traders to look for their first short position on the Microsoft stock.

We then see a pullback into an xBrat SlingShot zone and a daily resistance zone to find resistance before the price continues its way back down. A second entry was breaking the same support zone, and the previous 5* SELL signal was the obvious choice here. Then we get an xBratAlgo 6* SELL signal and yet another opportunity to go short on $MSFT.

The confluence of the second slingshot target zone and the daily support zone around the $135 price had to be the target for short sellers to take profit. Notice how the price tested this zone for six days!

SHORTING $MSFT DURING RUSSIAN INVASION OF UKRAINE

The pullback in the $MSFT stock price during the Russian invasion of Ukraine was more complex compared to the COVID-19 pullback since world politics played a greater role in shaping the market trends.

The war was on the doorstep of Europe, and investors were closely monitoring the situation. Any movement in the stock markets was indicative of how the geopolitical event was impacting the financial markets. $MSFT, being a global tech giant, was also affected by this event, which led to the stock prices falling. The pullback was not only limited to $MSFT but also affected other stocks in the tech sector and the broader market.

One of the key factors that impacted the $MSFT stock price during this event was the company's exposure to the European market. Europe is a crucial market for $MSFT, and any disturbance in the region can impact the company's financials. The uncertainties and risks associated with the Ukraine-Russia conflict led to a lack of investor enthusiasm and prompted them to pull out of investments in tech stocks, thereby lowering the stock prices. This was the catalyst that started the move, but it was then enhanced by an insider trade at the beginning of February, reducing risk and taking nearly $8.5 million when offloading many $MSFT shares.

These two confluences were great. Then, we had a test of a daily resistance zone (first blue ellipse on Chart 8.7), and resistance was found in a slingshot probability pullback zone and a type 1 and 2 SELL signal. We had a confluence of a geopolitical event, insider activity, technical structural test/rejection, and a technical strategy signal. My first trade found support at the first slingshot target zone, then the price went back into the pullback zone and tested it again. Then, at the second test and rejection of the slingshot first target zone, a double bottom formed, confirming strong support and making this a sensible opportunity for me to take profit on this short trade.

Moving along, I ignored the 5* and 6* BUY signals for the xBrat Algo in the first red ellipse. These signals occur just before the resistance zone, and we don't go long into resistance. The zone did hold at the second blue ellipse, and the price returned to a bearish pullback trend. I ignored the 6* SELL signal as not too much fresh air was present before the weekly support zone formed from the double bottom during the first trade's support at the slingshot target zone. This support did hold after the 6* SELL and resulted in a strong confluence catalyst for the bounce up into a new slingshot pullback zone and a new daily resistance zone.

Despite the weekly support zone being present just below, the slingshot type 2 sell is taken as we have confluence of 6* SELL, which we didn't take. A slingshot sell signal and the formation of this new daily resistance zone in the slingshot pullback zone are notable. Too many stars were aligned to ignore, and it seemed likely that the weekly support would break and go lower with more confluences happening for the bearish momentum. The yellow hashed lines and arrow mark the second short trade on $MSFT. Target 2 is always my last target for these shorts, as that's where my probability zones lead.

The third red ellipse and 6* SELL signal are ignored as we don't short into support. We got a bullish pullback in June and July, helped by decent earnings, but it wasn't enough to break up the new daily resistance zone we used for the second trade.

The next xBratAlgo 6* SELL signal (remember, a confluence of 12 out of 12 points of control) breaks through and closes through the weekly resistance zone, leading us to the third short trading opportunity (purple hashed line and arrow). The trade moved in the same direction as the weekly Wave 4 profit taking pullback, with lots of fresh air to the next support zone and plenty of time before the next earnings call. The last red ellipse is the slingshot sell signal, which did get to target 2. I didn't take it since the weekly timeframe we were in with the red Elliott Wave pullback zone with weekly volume was waning.

With three good shorts and funds available, my focus shifted, and I started looking for this support to hold and

Chart 8.7 – Shorting $MSFT During Russian Invasion of Ukraine.

then confluences to align for the opportunity to add to my $MSFT investment positions.

ADDING TO $MSFT POSITIONS

Always be more cautious when you are adding to your investment positions after a pullback. Looking for momentum led by confluences is key, specifically multiple long signals, support holding, and positive earnings calls, to name a few. Going back to Chart 8.5, which is the weekly chart of $MSFT, Wave 4 found support, but being patient for a break of the last weekly resistance just below $280 is paramount.

Chart 8.8 is a daily chart that continues from the previously outlined 2023 shorts with bullish momentum building. We get four slingshot bullish signals, three of which post earnings in January. The last is a type 3 BUY going into my final weekly resistance zone decision point. The blue dash-dot line was the entry and a good few weeks before the next earnings call at the end of April. Price did come down into another slingshot support and probability pullback zone just before earnings and then gapped up and really took hold to the upside.

CONCLUSION

When investing, confluence needs to form from a multitude of instances and show that bullish momentum is building. Think of it like a main bullish river getting fed by more and more tributaries, and these confluences are so strong that the next share-buying exercise takes place.

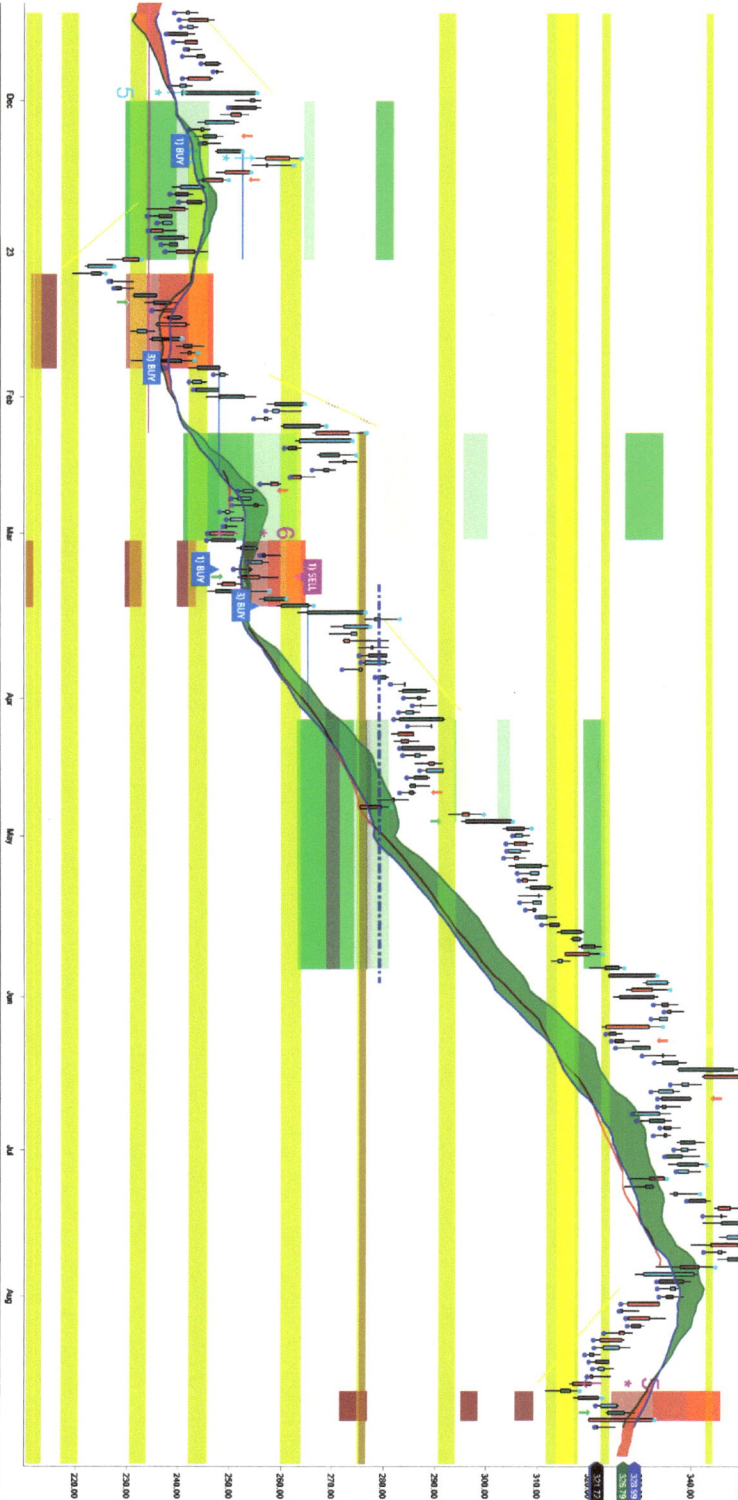

Chart 8.8 – Adding To $MSFT Shareholding with Profits for Previous Shorts.

SECTION 4

CONCLUSION AND NEXT STEPS

CHAPTER 9

Concluding Thoughts on Financial Market Confluences

CONFLUENCES ARE THE points at which various market indicators and signals intersect, creating an unignorable convergence of information that can guide trading and investing decisions. These confluences can occur across all types of trading instruments, including stocks, bonds, commodities, and currencies. Additionally, confluences can be observed across different trading strategies, from day trading to swing trading to long-term investing.

The key to identifying confluences is to take a step back and observe the market from a distance before diving in. This approach can help traders see patterns and trends that may not be evident at first glance. As more and more confluences start to appear, traders can begin to focus on specific indicators and signals.

Of course, identifying confluences takes practice and skill. That's why many traders rely on specialized software to do some of the heavy lifting for them. This type of financial software can analyse vast amounts of market data and highlight the most significant confluences, allowing traders to make informed decisions in a fraction of the time.

One important aspect of confluences is their ability to tell a story. By examining different market indicators and watching how they interact with one another, traders can start to develop a narrative about where the market is headed. This story can help traders make more confident and accurate trading and investing decisions. The confluences themselves become the catalyst for this narrative, providing the elements upon which the story is built.

For the most part, trading is a solitary business. Oftentimes, you don't have colleagues with whom to discuss the story. Something I always say to the traders I meet is, "Don't be afraid to tell yourself the story of the behaviour and confluences. Say it out loud." If you actually speak and hear it, it will make more sense and may even keep you out of a trade.

NEXT STEPS

Throughout this book, I have presented numerous examples of confluences in action. Through detailed analysis and real-life case studies, the book demonstrates how traders can use confluences to their advantage. Even better, because confluences repeatedly occur, finding examples is pretty straightforward. By studying these examples and mastering the art of identifying confluences, you can take your trading strategies to the next level.

If you're ready to jump in, read on. I've summarized the main concepts discussed throughout the book and will now provide some specific steps to help you get started identifying confluences and trading for greater success.

CONFLUENCE CHECKLISTS

A checklist is a good starting point and can help traders and investors develop their "confluence muscle memory." A simple and repeatable process can be learned quickly. To get you started, I have put together confluence checklists for day trading and swing trading. As you will see, there are two separate lists for each method of trading.

Big-Picture View

This list is where you should begin. It outlines specific steps and actions to take in order to develop a big-picture understanding. Once these basics have become second nature, you can move on to the next list.

Targeted View

Begin this list after you understand and have mastered the big-picture approach. The targeted approach adds complexity and depth to the big picture by adding multiple technical indicators to the equation. The additional findings provide a deeper dive into the details.

DAY TRADING STARTERS

Confluence day trading in financial markets requires careful planning, risk management, and a thorough understanding of technical analysis. By following these checklists, traders can increase their chances of success and minimize their risk exposure in the market.

Confluences should flow in the same direction. Additionally, traders must ensure that all confluences align in the same direction. This means that all factors, such as indicators, levels, and trends, should point towards the same trade direction. If only one factor contradicts the overall flow, it is best not to take the trade. This point is crucial. It highlights the importance of patience and discipline in trading, which can ultimately lead to better returns.

Remember, choosing one instrument and becoming intimate with everything surrounding this instrument and the confluences at play is easier than trying to trade using two or more.

BIG-PICTURE VIEW

1. Frame your charts with key support and resistance zones from the native timeframe you are trading and the 15-minute, 30-minute, and 60-minute timeframes. Also, be sure to include major trend channels for higher timeframes.

2. Add EMA clouds to your charts. As mentioned, to get you started, I've included an EMA Cloud Indicator tool free with the purchase of this book. This can be accessed via the QR code on the right. For day trading, 21 EMA and 34 EMA are great starting points.

3. Look for economic data points and news. Your first action at the beginning of each week is to have a precise view of what data could affect your instrument. Additionally, keep an eye on world news beyond the financial world. It is just as important and can have a big impact on investments.

TARGETED VIEW

1. Set a solid foundation by having the big-picture view established.

2. Add more detail to your charts. Use multiple technical indicators rather than relying on just one. Remember, confluences from different strategies can converge to solidify directional

Scan me!

Introducing the
FREE xBrat EMA Cloud Indicator

Check out all the trading platforms the **xBrat EMA Cloud Indicator** is available for, by scanning the QR Code above

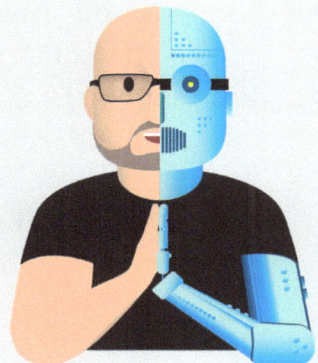

trading decisions, which makes them very powerful. I would advise not overloading your charts but rather choosing two or three max that will complement each other.

3. Continue to update support and resistance zones on the native timeframe during the trading day. If a price tests a support or resistance zone three or more times, it's important!

4. Manage your risk. Day traders should always set stop losses to control risk exposure. Look for a sensible placement for the stop loss order that takes into consideration the confluences of recent pivots and other structural factors.

5. DO NOT be greedy. If there is a confluence of structural factors and/or upcoming economic data points, this is significant and should be your target timing to take profit.

SWING TRADING STARTERS

Confluence swing trading is more complex than day trading, with more macro factors at play. It may take a little more work to set up, but taking the time to set yourself up for success is crucial. To take advantage of high-probability swing trading opportunities, you need to understand the whole picture and identify both fundamental and technical confluences.

To simplify this complex process, I developed the xBrat Stocks Predator software, which specifically hunts down confluences from many data sources to make light work of trying to gather and sift through all the data available online and individually through other software.

For short-term swing trading, choose one instrument and become intimate with everything surrounding this instrument and the confluences at play. For medium-term swing trading, select a maximum of five stocks and do the same thing. The daily timeframe allows more time to understand behaviour for medium- and longer-term strategies.

BIG-PICTURE VIEW

1. Frame your charts with key support and resistance zones from the native timeframe you are trading and the 30-minute, 60-minute, daily and weekly timeframes. Also, be sure to include major trend channels for higher timeframes.
2. Add EMA clouds to your charts. As mentioned, to get you started, I've included an EMA Cloud Indicator tool free with the purchase of this book. This can be accessed via the QR code on the right. For swing trading, 55 EMA and 89 EMA are great starting points.

Scan me!

Introducing the
**FREE xBrat
EMA
Cloud
Indicator**

Check out all the trading platforms the **xBrat EMA Cloud Indicator** is available for, by scanning the QR Code above

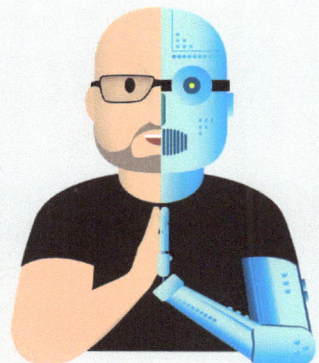

3. For short-term swing trading, look for economic data points and news. Your first action at the beginning of each week is to have a precise view of what data could affect your instrument. Remember not to carry trades over the weekend — getting in a trade on a Friday is not advisable.
4. For each of your stocks, pay close attention to the earnings calendar, news, insider activity, and unusual options activity — on a daily and weekly basis.

TARGETED VIEW

1. Set a solid foundation by having the big-picture view established.
2. Add more detail to your charts. Use multiple technical indicators rather than relying on just one. Remember, confluences from different strategies can converge to solidify directional trading decisions, which makes them very powerful. I would advise not overloading your charts but rather choosing two or three max that will complement each other.
3. Continue to update support and resistance zones on the native timeframe during the week. If a price tests a support or resistance zone three or more times, it's important!
4. Manage your risk. Swing traders should always set stop losses to control risk exposure. Look for a sensible placement for the stop loss order that takes into consideration the confluences of recent pivots and other structural factors.
5. DO NOT be greedy. If there is a confluence of structural factors and/or upcoming earnings, this is significant and should be your target timing to take profit.

FINAL THOUGHTS

Remember to be patient and disciplined, and always consider all factors before executing a trade. I approach it this way: if all factors are converging, with confluences flowing in the same direction, and I can't find that reason, then the trade, by default, is high probability. When I encounter these confluences, a burning question arises within me. How many other traders have spotted them and are taking action now or devising strategies for the present or future?

However, do not dwell on missed trades; just learn from them. Look backwards and wider to see if you missed any confluence factors, and take notes for next time. There is always room to widen the checklist. It's just a starting point.

And, while it may seem counterintuitive, I always look for reasons NOT TO TRADE!

My hope with this book is that traders of all levels, even those who are just beginning to consider entering the world of trading and investing, will develop a heightened awareness of confluences.

The confluences that have brought you to read this book are derived from your own life experiences and, for some, experiences in the financial markets. In trading and investing, there exists no magical solution, only the patience to learn and a receptive mindset to recognize confluence and patterns.

About Paul (xBrat)

PAUL BRATBY, an accomplished ex-British Army engineering manager, possesses a unique talent for recognizing behavioural patterns and finding intersections between human behaviour and the financial markets. Through a series of remarkable life events, Paul has progressed from a humble 17-year-old apprentice in the British Army to a successful trader who founded Global Trading Software and its popular series of trading indicator software.

After completing his military service, Paul yearned for the excitement that it brought. From 2011 to 2013, he found himself in Afghanistan and West Africa, working as a contractor. Even in those challenging environments, he managed to trade the financial markets via satellite internet connections.

In 2013, as technology was improving, Paul embarked on a new journey. His focus shifted to transforming intricate trading and investing strategies into user-friendly software. The goal? To simplify the trading process with clear visualizations and easily understandable rules that would be accessible to traders of all levels.

With this mission accomplished, his first book becomes a testament to his expertise and serves as a stepping stone in his ongoing quest to share knowledge and experiences with others. Paul attributes his triumphs to his steadfast adherence to disciplined rules and his unwavering commitment to rational decision-making in both life and trading.

This book was written at Paul's Spanish residence. He and his wife, Dee, spend summers there, seeking respite from the sweltering heat of Dubai, which they proudly call home.

CONTACT PAUL:

WEBSITES: GlobalTradingSoftware.com/
PaulBratby.com/

SOCIAL: X (Formerly Twitter) Twitter.com/PBratbyOfficial

YOUTUBE: youtube.com/@GTSTradingIndicators

Paul and his trading team run an exclusive
40-week Apprenticeship program teaching traders the
trading strategies associated with all the software
mentioned in this book and combines them for his
Confluence Trading Strategies for Day Trading and Swing Trading.

Scan the QR code for more information.

Scan me!

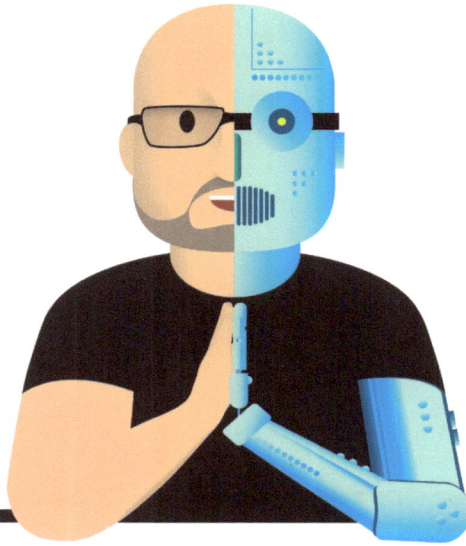

As gratitude for purchasing my book, I would like to give you
2 of my trading software titles that I mention in this book.

Simply Scan the QR code below for more information.

Scan me!

The **xBrat Guardian zones** were mentioned throughout the book. The software algorithm automatically plots multiple timeframe support and resistance zones on a traders chart.

Scan the QR code for more information.

Scan me!

True Story

I'D LIKE TO tell you a true story about an exchange of emails that happened whilst I was writing this book during the summer of 2023. One could say it was a life confluence between another trader and me. The trader emailed me in response to a series of "Get to Know Paul Bratby" emails that were sent to new software customers. The email shared how confluences in my life led me to trading and put me on track to be successful. I have changed the individual's name for privacy purposes, so let's call him Kevin.

As you've probably learned by this point, confluences occur when two or more factors align and drive financial market movement. These powerful indicators and patterns are largely driven by human behaviour. In a rapidly changing market environment, investors tend to behave in predictable ways, leading to the formation of specific trading patterns.

My emails with Kevin summarize a lot of my beliefs and understandings. Most notably, our interaction highlights my ability to see patterns in human behaviour, identify the probable confluences that lead to this behaviour, and predict potential paths leading forward.

It's important to note that I have not changed in any way the grammar or spelling in the trader's emails or in mine, and I will comment on this after you have read through the email exchange.

My comments on this email exchange will follow the emails.

KEVIN'S FIRST EMAIL:

"Hi Paul,

I would like to thank you for offering me your help

I have been trading for twenty years.I started out with safety in the market W.D. Gahn Elliotte wave Jesse liver more. Price action candlesticks Financial Astrology.Volume indicators time of sales etc

They all have a place in the market, even the 50 ema 200ema. It all works.

You are right it takes years to learn all of this and to act emotionless and sit in front of the computer day in day out, but thats how i do trading .

Practice practice. Practice no magic pill makes you a trader

Paul you where in the military so let me ask you.

would you go to war with a gun without knowing every part how it works to the point that you put on a blind fold and know what and why it able to work .Down to even hand loading your own Ammunition each and every Bullet so you know the correct trajectory???

well that's how i trade pressing a button because someone programs a computer with magic indicators wont work for a real trader they have to know how and what

I can tell you all of the tools i have mentioned above work .but the trader has to know how far the target is to allow for accurate placement after knowing the gun works.i was interested until i heard it was anoyher progrom like the other 10000s for sale that i have to spend money to learn then hope Hope it works without knowing how and what it does sure Multiple time entrys on fibb works bur theres more lots more .if you are telling me you can give away your 20 years of traing to me for a thousand dollars there's something wrong

I attended a ███████████ weekend seminar where he offered me a job at the end of it cause all my magic showed him how accurate it is he offered me a six figure salary to work with him .

I worked so hard I couldn't sell it for that.

I'm sure you're not giving your system away for any less."

MY RESPONSE, AFTER A COUPLE OF DAYS TO THINK CLEARLY:

"Hi Kevin

I appreciate your military analogy and your dedication to understanding every part of the gun, including hand-loading your own ammunition.

As a seasoned soldier and engineering manager with 15 years of service in the British Army, I can attest to the importance of maintaining a weapon for optimal performance. The process of stripping and cleaning a gun was considered crucial in ensuring its functionality; however, detailed knowledge of its inner workings was not an essential part of our training. Any malfunctioning weapons were handled by specialist Armourers rather than the average soldier. The soldier's focus was to be directed carrying out tasks required on the battlefield, and so, detailed knowledge of inner workings could be viewed as an unnecessary burden, slowing down the individual's performance.

Similarly, the evolution of weapon technology has further simplified the previously time-consuming task of loading magazines. From the process of loading magazines one bullet at a time, we have advanced to automatic loaders that significantly reduce loading times. All that is required is to take the device out of the box and apply it to the magazine, thus enabling rapid loading of 20 rounds instantaneously. As a failsafe measure, we would ensure that the top round was seated correctly before proceeding to the next task. It is essential to note that technological advancements have had a significant impact on the battlefield, evolving the way the military carries out their duties.

The highest quality of any military personnel is their obedience to orders and guidelines. In warfare, following these principles is often more critical than having extensive knowledge about the inner workings of a weapon. Victory in war is not the product of emotion; rather, it is won through tactical adherence to commands and strict rule-following. Therefore, in summary, while detailed knowledge of how weapons work is essential in repairing and maintaining them, the focus should be on carrying out the necessary tasks to win the war.

However, when it comes to trading, the landscape has changed significantly. Just like how technology has revolutionized various industries, it has also transformed trading.

In the past, traders had to rely on laborious calculations and technical analysis to identify complex patterns and completion zones in the markets. However, now algorithms and software can perform these calculations and present them in a visually understandable format on a chart. This doesn't mean that traders can simply press a button and rely on magic indicators to make all of their trading decisions; rather, traders need to have a deeper understanding of trading principles.

This includes knowing how to interpret the completion zones on a chart, but more importantly, when to trade or not trade on this information. One essential skill is identifying both linear and non-linear support and resistance zones, which can help traders avoid making erroneous trades. For example, traders should not short into support.

I appreciate that you have found success using various tools and methods in your 20 years of trading. However, it's essential to recognize that the trading landscape has evolved dramatically, and we need to change with it to remain competitive and successful.

As an experienced trader and former money manager, I have always been focused on building wealth not just for myself, but for future generations of my family. However, I also saw the vast potential to be of value to the millions of retail traders around the world who struggle to achieve success in the markets. That's why, nine years ago, I embarked on a personal mission to harness my extensive experience and knowledge into software that could simplify and streamline the trading process.

Working alongside a team of talented coders, I developed a range of innovative indicators and tools that have helped close to 20,000 traders across the globe to refine their trading strategies and achieve greater financial freedom. Each of our indicators and tools have been meticulously designed to aid traders in making more informed, accurate trading decisions - and the feedback we've received has been overwhelmingly positive.

With a team of over 20 staff members in locations around the world, we've been able to empower traders like never before. Our focus on simplicity and ease-of-use has enabled even novice traders to make sense of the complex world of trading, and our affordable pricing means that our software is accessible to traders at every level of experience.

Overall, our software has been a game-changing addition to the world of trading, creating jobs and growing the industry, whilst providing traders with a new level of simplicity and profitability. I'm proud of the work we've done, and excited to see what the future holds for our growing community of traders.

I feel that I give value to the trading world and not think too much of what my value is."

KEVIN'S REPLY:

"Paul

I am honoured and Thankyou for spending the time to write to me and help me appreciate the true passion you have for trading as I do

Most people only come to trading to make money ,yes of course it's the end resolve but my personality as of my many years of running my own self made business

I only found success by having total control and understanding of every detail

I have caught you on face book and I could see your genuine attitude to not only wanting to help people of all levels learn to be financial independent and have there own income stream

I know that I have times where trading becomes lonely and tiering work

Paul I'm grateful you are reaching out to me and in no way am I wanting to offend you and I apologise if you feel I am as no malice is intended

But I have to know how sincere you are to really support your product and as you said I have to trust your magazine before I'm put in the firing line

I will go over your videos and yes I believe in you I just needed this e-mail from you

I want to grow and adapt in trading so yes I am interested Thankyou"

MY THOUGHTS

So, initially, I can tell that Kevin's emails were written on a mobile phone, as these sorts of spelling mistakes are a common theme when I use my fat fingers to type on my own phone. One example of this is typing "anoyher" instead of "another" because on the keyboard, the letter "y" is next to "t." It's almost written like a text message, where that pesky predictive autocorrect text gets in the way.

Kevin may have been in a rush, not at home on his computer. This tells me he felt strongly about replying to my email straight away, which made me take some time to think about my reply so that I could help him understand a little more about me and how the software helps.

Also, notice how more relaxed the second email was from Kevin. There are fewer spelling mistakes, but it was still written on a phone (the punctuation and grammar still read like a text message). It is less intense and more reflective.

Sometimes, when people have been doing something for a long time, they simply miss (or ignore) the opportunities to allow advances in technology to do the heavy lifting for them. Whilst I'm absolutely confident that Kevin is a competent trader, it's very difficult these days to collect all the data, catalysts, and confluences in the market without technology.

It's also no longer necessary to get bogged down with trying to understand every technical measurement, data input, and reaction. There's been a lot of money spent on developing trading and investing software, and experts with lots of experience have written the well-known rules and logical outcomes of many external factors that affect markets. This has even included training AI on how past confluences have affected markets in order to try to predict the probabilities of similar outcomes happening again. Very clever young people have turned that knowledge into code with outcomes that match the rules, and this is then backtested thoroughly before being released.

The good thing about all this technology is that traders of all levels can add it to their charts and simply look left on the charts and backtest it themselves to build confidence.

The experiences that have brought me to this exact moment in my life have been diverse, but it all began with my resolute decision to enlist in the British Army. Possessing the necessary discipline to adhere to strict rules without hesitation or objection has served as a pinnacle contributor to the successes I've had throughout my trading career.

Additionally, I have always maintained a flexible mindset when it comes to identifying patterns and crucial turning points — confluences — that can arise in life. Embracing change is a fundamental concept for progression, which has allowed me to seamlessly evolve my approach as I navigate the complex, ever-changing landscapes within the world of trading and investing.

I hope that Kevin continues to communicate with me so I can help him navigate a new potential path in his trading career. And I hope that the confluences that led Kevin and me to communicate will have a positive outcome.

Trading Terms

HERE ARE SOME of the main trading terms you will encounter as you read the book. I have filtered out the fluff and concentrated on what I think is important. You can reference these terms if you are struggling with any of the information.

Ask – In trading and investing, the ask is the amount a party is willing to sell in order to buy a financial instrument.

Bearish – Being bearish in trading means you believe that a market, asset, or financial instrument is going to experience a downward trajectory. Being bearish is the opposite of being bullish, which means that you think the market is heading upwards.

Bid – In trading and investing, the bid is the amount a party is willing to pay in order to buy a financial instrument.

Bullish – Bullish traders believe, based on their analysis, that a market will experience an upward price movement. Being bullish involves buying an underlying market in order to profit by selling the market in the future once the price has risen.

Broker – A broker is an independent company that organises and executes financial transactions on behalf of traders. They can do this across a number of different asset classes, including stocks, forex, futures, and cryptocurrencies. A broker will normally charge a commission for the order to be executed.

Candlestick – A candlestick is a type of price chart used in technical analysis that displays the high, low, open, and closing prices of a security for a specific period.

Closing Price – A closing price is the last level at which an asset was traded before the market closed on any given day. Closing prices are often used as a marker when looking at movements over a longer term. They can be compared to previous closing prices or the opening price to measure an asset's movement over a single day. The closing price of individual candlesticks intraday is also used in the same way to understand behaviours in any given market over any given time period.

Currency Future – A currency future is a contract that details the price at which a currency could be bought or sold and sets a specific date for the exchange.

Day Trading – Day trading is a strategy of short-term investment that involves closing out all trades before the market closes.

Exchange – An exchange is an open, organised marketplace for commodities, stocks, securities, derivatives, and other financial instruments. The terms exchange and market are often used interchangeably, as they both describe an environment in which listed products can be traded.

Execution – In trading, execution is the completion of a buy or sell order from a trader. It is carried out by a broker.

Federal Reserve – The Federal Reserve Bank, or the "Fed" for short, is the central bank in charge of monetary and financial stability in the United States. It is part of a wider system — known as the Federal Reserve system — with 12 regional central banks located in major cities across the US.

Fibonacci Retracement – A Fibonacci retracement is a key technical analysis tool that uses percentages and horizontal lines drawn onto price charts to identify possible areas of support and resistance. Identifying these areas is useful to traders since it can help them decide when to open and close a position or when to apply stops and limits to their trades.

Fill – Fill is the term used to refer to the satisfying of an order to trade a financial asset. It is the basic act of any market transaction — when an order has been completed, it is often referred to as filled or having been executed. However, it is worth noting that there is no guarantee that every trade will become filled.

FOMC – FOMC stands for the Federal Open Market Committee, which is the branch of the Federal Reserve responsible for reviewing and overseeing open market operations in the US. Through intervening in open market operations — buying or selling government securities — the FOMC can indirectly change the federal funds rate.

Forex – Forex is how market participants convert one currency to another. It can variously be referred to as foreign exchange, FX, or currencies.

Fundamental Analysis – Fundamental analysis is a method of evaluating the intrinsic value of an asset and analysing the factors that could influence its price in the future. This form of analysis is based on external events and influences, as well as financial statements and industry trends.

Futures Contract – Futures contracts represent an agreement between two parties to trade an asset at a defined price on a specified date in the future. They are also often referred to simply as futures.

GDP – GDP stands for gross domestic product or the total value of the goods and services produced in a country over a specified period. It is used as an indicator of the size and health of a country's economy.

Heikin Ashi – Heikin Ashi is a type of chart pattern used in technical analysis. Heikin Ashi charts are similar to candlestick charts, but the main difference is that a Heikin Ashi chart uses the daily price averages to show the median price movement of an asset. The xBratAlgo trading strategy indicator is designed using Heikin Ashi charting.

Limit Order – A limit order is an instruction to your broker to execute a trade at a particular level that is more favourable than the current market price.

Long Position – When used in trading, long refers to a position that makes a profit if an asset's market price increases. Usually used in context as "taking a long position" or "going long."

Margin – In trading, margin is the amount of funds required to open and maintain a leveraged position. For example, if you wanted to trade one contract of NQ Futures, a trader would need $12,500 available cash in his/her account to act as margin to trade the one contract.

Market Data – Market data refers to the live streaming of trade-related data. It encompasses a range of information, such as price, bid/ask quotes, and market volume. Trading venues provide reports on various assets and financial instruments, which are then distributed to traders and firms. Market data is available across thousands of global markets, including stocks, indexes, forex, and commodities. It is provided by each broker, and sometimes there is a monthly charge for this.

Market Order – A market order is an instruction from a trader to a broker to execute a trade immediately at the best available price.

MACD – The moving average convergence/divergence (MACD) is a technical analysis indicator that aims to identify changes in a share price's momentum. The MACD collects data from different moving averages to help traders identify possible opportunities around support and resistance levels.

Moving Average – A moving average (often shortened to MA) is a common indicator in technical analysis used to examine the price movements of assets while lessening the impact of random price spikes.

NFP – Non-farm payrolls are a monthly statistic representing how many people are employed in the United States in manufacturing, construction, and goods companies. They are also referred to as non-farms or NFPs.

Open – Open has a couple of definitions within investing. It can refer to the daily opening of an exchange and an order or position that has not yet been filled or closed.

Open Positions – An open position is a trade that is still able to generate a profit or incur a loss. When a position is closed, all profits and losses are realised, and the trade is no longer active. Open positions can be either long or short, enabling you to profit from markets rising as well as falling.

Option – An option is a financial instrument that offers you the right, but not the obligation, to buy or sell an asset when its price moves beyond a certain price within a set time period.

Order – In trading, an order is a request sent to a broker or trading platform to make a trade on a financial instrument.

Pip – A pip is a measurement of movement in forex trading, defined as the smallest move that a currency can make.

Position – A position is the expression of a market commitment, or exposure, held by a trader. It is the financial term for a trade that is either currently able to incur a profit or a loss (known as an open position) or a trade that has recently been cancelled (known as a closed position). Profit or loss on a position can only be realised once it has been closed.

Pullback – A pullback is a temporary pause or dip in an asset's overall trend. The term is sometimes used interchangeably with "retracement" or "consolidation." However, a pullback should not be confused with a reversal, which is a more permanent move against the prevailing trend.

Rally – A rally is a period in which the price of an asset sees sustained upward momentum. Typically, a rally will occur after a period in which prices have been flat, trading in a narrow band, or experiencing a decline.

Range – Range is the difference between a market's highest and lowest price in a given period. It is mostly used as an indicator of volatility: if a market has a wide range, it's a sign that it was volatile over the period analysed.

Resistance Zone – A resistance zone is a small range on a price chart at which an upward price trajectory is impeded by an overwhelming inclination to sell the asset. If a market price is nearing a resistance zone, a trader may opt to close their position and take the profit rather than risk the price falling back.

Reversal – A reversal is a turnaround in the price movement of an asset: when an upward trend (a rally) becomes a downward one (a correction) or vice versa. They are also often referred to as trend reversals.

Risk Management – Risk management is the process of identifying potential risks in your investment portfolio and taking steps to mitigate accordingly.

Risks – In trading, risks are the ways in which an investment can end up losing you money.

Rollover – In trading, a rollover is the process of keeping a position open beyond its expiry. In futures trading, it is the process of rolling over the contract instrument to the next contract period.

Scalping – Scalping in trading is the act of opening and then closing a position very quickly in the hopes of profiting from small price movements.

Sectors – Sectors are divisions within an economy or market. They are useful for analysing performance or comparing companies with similar outputs and characteristics.

Short – In trading, short describes a trade that will incur a profit if the asset being traded falls in price. It is also often referred to as going short, shorting, or sometimes selling.

Slippage – When the price at which an order is executed does not match the price at which it was made, it is referred to as slippage.

Spread – In finance, spread is the difference in price between the buy (bid) and sell (offer) prices quoted for an asset.

Stop Order – Stop orders are types of orders that instruct your broker to execute a trade when it reaches a particular price level, generally one that is less favourable than the current market price. They can also be known as stop-loss orders.

Straddle – A straddle in trading is a type of options strategy. It allows traders to speculate on whether a market is about to become volatile without having to predict a specific price movement. It involves either buying or selling simultaneous call and put options with matching strike prices and expiration dates.

Support Zone – A support zone is a small range on a price chart at which a downward price trajectory is impeded by an overwhelming inclination to buy the asset. If a market price is nearing a support zone, a trader may opt to close their short position and take the profit rather than risk the price rising back.

Technical Analysis – Technical analysis is a means of examining and predicting price movements in the financial markets by using historical price charts and market statistics. It is based on the idea that if a trader can identify previous market patterns, they can form a fairly accurate prediction of future price trajectories.

Trailing Stop – A trailing stop is a type of stop-loss that follows positive market movements of an asset you are trading.

If your position moves favourably but then reverses, a trailing stop can lock in your profits and close the position. These can be placed and adjusted manually as the trade progresses or automatically with an automated trading strategy.

Trend – In the world of trading and investing, trend refers to the overarching direction in which a particular asset or market is moving. Trends can be short- or long-term and may be influenced by factors such as economic indicators, news events, and market sentiment. Understanding trends is a crucial component of successful trading and investing, allowing traders to capitalize on opportunities while mitigating risks.

VIX – VIX is short for the Chicago Board Options Exchange's CBOE Volatility Index. It is a measure used to track volatility on the S&P 500 index and is the most well-known volatility index on the markets.

Volatility – A market's volatility is its likelihood of making major, unforeseen short-term price movements at any given time.

Volume – In trading, volume is the amount of a particular asset that is being traded over a certain period of time. It is often presented alongside price information as it offers an extra dimension when examining an asset's price history.

VWAP – VWAP is the abbreviation for volume-weighted average price, which is a technical analysis tool that shows the ratio of an asset's price to its total trade volume. It provides traders and investors with a measure of the average price at which a stock is traded over a given period of time.

www.ingramcontent.com/pod-product-compliance
Lightning Source LLC
Chambersburg PA
CBHW041159220326
41597CB00001BA/3